Project Manager's Spotlight on

Planning

CATHERINE A. TOMCZYK, PMP

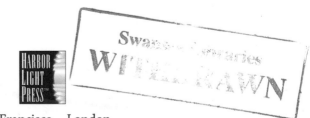

HARBOR
LIGHT
PRESS™

San Francisco   London

Publisher: Neil Edde
Acquisitions Editor: Heather O'Connor
Developmental Editor: Maureen Adams
Production Editor: Leslie E.H. Light
Technical Editor: Mike Nollet
Copyeditor: Kim Wimpsett
Compositor: Maureen Forys and Jeff Wilson, Happenstance Type-O-Rama
Graphic Illustrator: Jeff Wilson, Happenstance Type-O-Rama
Proofreaders: Jim Brook, Amy McCarthy, Nancy Riddiough
Indexer: Nancy Guenther
Book Designer: Maureen Forys, Happenstance Type-O-Rama
Cover Designer and Illustrator: Daniel Ziegler, Ziegler Design

Library of Congress Card Number: 2005920771

ISBN: 0-7821-4413-6

Manufactured in the United States of America

10 9 8 7 6 5 4 3 2 1

To our valued readers,

Harbor Light Press was created as an imprint of Sybex, Inc. to help business professionals acquire the practical skills and knowledge they need to meet today's most pressing business challenges.

Our books serve the people responsible for getting the job done— project managers charged with delivering a product on time and under budget; human resource directors faced with a complex array of resource decisions; support staff determined to exceed the goals set for them; and others who recognize that great business plans are only as good as the people who implement and manage them.

Harbor Light Press is committed to publishing authoritative, reliable, yet engaging business books written by authors who are outstanding instructors and experienced business professionals. The goal for all of our books is to connect with our readers, to understand their needs, and to provide them with solutions that they can put to use immediately.

Neil Edde
Publisher
Harbor Light Press

For Mikayla and Merlin, my biggest supporters

Contents

Foreword

The Project Manager's Spotlight Series is written for those of you who are engaged in projects at the day-to-day level of business. You're working on projects such as server consolidation, piloting new products in the marketplace, or opening a new branch or storefront. These day-to-day projects keep businesses moving forward, carving out market share, meeting strategic goals, and improving the firm's bottom line. These projects, while vitally important to the companies you work for, are not necessarily multi-million dollar, multi-year projects that require meticulous disciplines and precise methodologies.

The Project Manager's Spotlight Series shows you the how-to's of project management on a practical level. These books help you apply solid principles of project management without the rigor. You'll find tools, tips, and techniques to help you use Project Management Institute–based practices in your small- to medium-sized projects; these are tips you can read over the weekend and be ready and able to apply on Monday morning.

—Kim Heldman

Acknowledgments

I didn't know how many people it took to create a book. Now I understand why the people at the Oscars can't keep their thank-you lists short and sweet. Several people supported me in countless ways during the process of writing this book. The following are in order of appearance.

I want to start by thanking Ron Thompson for introducing me to Kim Heldman. Kim was instrumental in creating the idea behind the Spotlight Series and pushing it to fruition. As a writer, sometimes you're frustrated, confused, and wordless; Kim was always there for help and encouragement, even while she was in bed with pneumonia. She's a pillar of strength if I ever saw one. Thank you, Kim.

Heather O'Connor gave me the opportunity to write this book. She had a vision of what this book could be and set the stage for the tone and flow of not only this book but also the entire series. Maureen Adams stepped in as developmental editor when Heather went on leave. Maureen demonstrated great project management skills because she had to step into the middle of the project and get up to speed in a short period of time. Maureen helped me convey the message in a logical order with gentle, focused suggestions.

Mike Nollet was the technical editor who kept the terminology consistent throughout the book. His knowledge of the PMBOK was invaluable. Leslie Light, the production editor, was always enthusiastic and calming. She knew when to stand by patiently and when to push the project forward. Leslie's ideas always added a finishing touch to the book. Kim Wimpsett, the copy editor, is a master at asking the clarifying questions and making suggestions that kept the book flowing. I also want to thank the people at Happenstance Type-O-Rama who turned my rough drawings and templates into the clear figures that grace these pages.

My friends and family were my emotional cheerleaders. Your emotional support was priceless. And finally, I want to thank Merlin and Mikayla. My daughter, Mikayla, desperately wanted to contribute to this book. Unfortunately, her random keystrokes didn't add to the clarity of the message, and I had to edit them from the final product. Merlin, words are inadequate to express my love and appreciation for your support in this project. I love you both.

Introduction

P*roject Manager's Spotlight on Planning* was written for those of you who end up managing many projects and want to know if there's a better way. I've been managing projects in a variety of industries for more than 25 years. Most of the time, I had to manage 10–15 small-to-medium-sized projects simultaneously. I turned to project management books to glean hints to help calm the feeling of chaos. But I usually ended up smirking while reading and thinking to myself, "Yeah right, like I can follow all of those processes with all of my projects all of the time!" Over the years, what I've learned is that it's the discipline you learn while managing large projects that becomes the foundation for managing small projects.

The best foundation you can lay for any project is to give yourself and your project team time to create a project plan. Planning is the most important step for any project. It's the map you and your team will use to meet the expectations of the project stakeholders. I've found that a well-planned project requires less energy to manage than one that's based on crisis management. In addition, when you're pulled off to a new high-priority project, the other project can hum along to completion with minimal management. Notice I said *when*, not *if*. If you're managing small projects, you'll be given new priorities on a regular basis, and the only way you can ensure your other projects continue to work toward completion is to have a documented project plan that the team can use for scope reference.

The best approach to use while reading this book is to understand that I've given the complete best-practice approach for managing small-to-medium-sized projects. You need to know all the best practices in order to know which ones you can merge or truncate. You should review the project management plan templates in Appendix B while you read the chapters. Take notes on these pages, and revise these templates as necessary to create your project plan. Throw out what you can't use, build on what you choose to use, and share with your project manager comrades to continue to improve all your documentation.

At first, formal project methodology can be overwhelming. I recommend to you learn and embrace the entire process. Then you'll have the discipline engrained enough to decide which parts to keep and which parts to shelve. Keep in mind that the shelved items aren't usually shelved forever, as they may be useful on other projects. My hope is that you can use many of these templates to quickly improve the outcome of your project.

Each project has its own challenges, yet it also has familiar aspects. Your project management confidence will grow as you gain experience and see that the project management similarities outweigh the differences. Treat almost everything as a project—Saturday chores, kitchen remodeling, and fundraising activities—and all your life's projects will become easier to manage.

CHAPTER 1

Initiating the Project Plan

So, you want to be a project manager—or maybe you already are one. Either way, you continually end up doing projects as part of your job—nothing really big, just a bunch of small-to-medium-sized projects that eat up your days. You're most likely very good at organizing, getting things done, and managing multiple projects simultaneously. But you're always feeling a little behind the eight ball, frustrated by the time and energy you expend on these projects. This book will help you set up a planning methodology for small-to-medium-sized projects that will give you back time and energy while you continue to get your projects done on time and on budget. In this chapter, I'll describe the process for project initiating and introduce the project plan document. Project initiating is the steps you go through to get approval to even get started. This is when you first use resources to begin planning the project. But first, I'll define the types of projects—both small and large—you can work on and how their sizes can put constraints on planning.

Small vs. Large Projects

How do you decide whether you have a small or large project? You could easily say this book project is a small project. It's not just physically small, but it's *financially* small and on a short schedule whereas a retrofit of the San Francisco–Oakland Bay Bridge is a *large* project both physically and financially, and it's on a really long schedule. In this section, I'll discuss some of the differences between how Project Managers (PMs) manage small projects vs. large projects so you can determine which type of projects you may have been assigned.

In many ways, managing large projects is easier than managing small projects. For large projects, the PM is usually managing one major project at a time. It's easy to escalate and resolve issues on larger projects because the project is visible and many people understand the importance of the outcome. The team is usually dedicated to the project, and often bonuses are tied to the project's success. Large projects usually have formal procedures and reports for project management, including a charter; a cost-benefit analysis; a Strengths, Weaknesses, Opportunities, and Threats (SWOT) analysis; and a dedicated PM. With large projects, it is easier to dedicate the team's attention to brainstorming the project's risks and requirements, and your organization may even provide you with standard corporate benchmarks to help you plan.

In large projects, things are more defined than in small ones. Small projects seem to start with set due dates that don't allow for project initiating and planning time, which results in project management processes that combine Initiating and Planning. What this means to a PM is that while you are collecting information and getting formal approval to initiate the project, you are also planning how you will complete it. Resource assignment and documentation tend to start in a more casual way than they would in a large project. Large projects may start with documentation such as work orders, Statements of Work (SOW), sales orders, contract addendums, or service orders. These documents are usually standard company forms that define the requirements, deliverables, and estimates for size and delivery dates for the requested work. Project management is usually not as rigorous for small projects, and the expected turnaround is usually rather short.

Small projects are also temporary, are unique, and have a start and end date that meets the formal definition of a project. However, they're often overlooked as projects requiring project management discipline. This is because they often look *repeatable* because they have requirements that are similar to other projects. Projects that fall into this category are new products, new customer implementations, customer conversions, software releases, and annual events. It's critical that you jump on the project early and initiate project planning, or else the days will slip by, the end dates don't move, and you'll have to manage the project in chaos.

PMs who manage small projects are responsible for juggling and managing many projects in various stages of completion. The sponsor and team members are also involved in many projects. The sponsor may be a manager who is responsible for all projects of a certain type. Consequently, priorities may conflict, especially if the team is also responsible for production support or corrective maintenance. The corporate value of these projects is usually cumulative, so it's difficult to see the impact of missed schedules and budget overruns until year's end. Surprisingly, the attitude from management can often be, "Planning is a waste of time since we do these kinds of projects all the time." But this shouldn't be the case, and it's the job of the PM to reinforce the discipline pertaining to planning for the organization. After all, time spent planning up front will assure you a better chance of project success because the stakeholders and project team are all on the same page as far as the project goals and so on. It can potentially save you time in rework later as well as prevent the requirements from taking on a life of their own. How do you do that? Let's start with project initiating.

Initiating a Project

The beginning of a project is when an organization decides to do something new, such as create a product, a building, or an operation. This could be triggered by a market need, a customer request, or a government regulation. Who, what, where, when, how, and how much are just the beginning questions to ask about the project. Before you start planning the project, you need to complete the initiating, the first process group of the project life cycle. In the initiating phase of the project, the PM begins to collect answers to those and many more questions prior to the project kickoff. Let's discuss initiating in more detail.

Understanding the Initiating Process Group

In the *initiating* process group, someone (an individual in the organization, a group in an organization, or the organization itself) decides to do a project. How a project is initiated depends on the size of the project and your corporate process. Often there isn't a clear line of demarcation between the initiating and planning process groups. What's clear, however, is that a project needs to have a sponsor, some level of project definition, an approval to start, and a PM.

NOTE   If you need further explanation or a refresher on the standard project management processes, refer to Appendix A of this book.

All projects should have a *sponsor*: the person who ultimately has decision-making authority and who also has the responsibility over the project budget and the ability to assign resources. The sponsor can make your job easy or difficult depending on whether you can partner with them in managing the project or whether you have to spar with them on every step of the way. A strong, supportive sponsor can increase the credibility of your project and grant you authority over it.

TIP   As we all know, it isn't always possible to partner with your project sponsor. Sometimes the two of you will clash. As the PM, you'll need to bend to the sponsor's style to keep the project on track, which may involve, as we say in the business, "flexibility."

Sometimes you don't have a single sponsor; you have a *sponsor committee* or a group of managers responsible for prioritizing and managing the budgets of many projects. Sponsor committees add unnecessary complexity to every project because these committees can turn a simple decision into a major event.

TIP   If you have any influence, keep away from a sponsor committee situation and recruit a specific sponsor for your project.

How do PMs get assigned to projects? They may come to you in a variety of ways, both formal and informal. A formal project assignment may be a meeting with the sponsor and/or your boss where the sponsor explains the scope and expectations of the project and reviews all the project documentation. The project might also be assigned to you in an informal manner, such as through a conversation in a hallway or over lunch in the cafeteria. It all depends on how your organization operates.

The problem with a casual method of assignment is that you don't know your authority or responsibility over the project, and you can't be sure that the assignment is real. The main issue with these handoffs is that they often occur after project initiating, which is in your best interest as PM to be directly involved in. Should you jump on the project during planning based on a casual conversation? Probably not. If in doubt, go to your boss and verify the assignment.

TIP   I prefer to be identified as the PM early in the project so that I can be involved during initiating. Unfortunately, the PM selection is considered a deliverable of initiating, so oftentimes a PM doesn't enter the picture until the planning phase. My advice is to do your best to avoid being assigned to a project after initiating. Just know that sometimes you can't avoid it.

Preparing for Planning

During initiating of a small project, you need to get into the habit of planning projects within a day or two of your assignment, because you won't have the time or opportunity to delve into the planning of the projects once the projects have begun.

Before you start planning a project, take a few minutes for what I call "project manager reflection time." Give yourself some time to think through what you know and expect about the project before the rest of the project noise starts. The first time you do this, it may take a couple of hours. But after you practice and fine-tune this ability, it will take mere minutes. During this time, you'll find that you know more about the project than you thought you knew. I suspect after this exercise, you'll also have more confidence in your PM skills.

During reflection time, consider the resources your project requires, which departments will be involved, and the time it will take to complete the project, as well as the time your organization has allotted you to complete it. Consider also the Subject Matter Experts (SMEs) you may need to call on to help you with the project. And most important, consider how you'll communicate with your project team members.

You'll want to ask yourself dozens of questions. In the following sections, I present some sample questions to start your project reflection. I've also included the questions in a template format in Appendix B. As you practice this discipline and increase project management experience, you'll begin to collect your own questions. Even though this reflection time is for your benefit, as well as for your project's benefit, you'll want to keep the answers to these questions to yourself, as you wouldn't want to upset team members, stakeholders, or clients with your candor. The intent is that you may identify problems you may not want to share, such as potential sabotage or personal problems of a team member that you know may impact the project.

Process history Is there documentation from a similar project that you can use as a base? If you know of or have another similar project, immediately retrieve the documentation from the other project. Even if the other project was a disaster, start there. Expend your energy to improve the process and documentation rather than to create a new process. If there's no process in place, think about other processes your organization has in place and how you or your colleagues have achieved success in the past. I'll discuss options for creating processes in Chapter 7, "Defining the Quality Plan."

Project sponsor Consider your relationship with the project sponsor and whether you've worked well together in the past. If you've worked with this sponsor before, identify their strengths and weaknesses. Is the sponsor committed to this project, or is this just another task dumped on her plate? Does your sponsor have leverage in case you need additional resources or a clarification of priorities? Do you have a sponsor committee that will make the decisions? If you don't have a sponsor, do you need one, or do you have authority to make the necessary decisions? If you need a sponsor, whom do you want, and what is your plan to recruit one?

Resources Resources include labor, equipment, and materials. List what you know you'll need and what you suspect you'll need to complete the project. Is your team going to be spread across the globe? How will you have meetings? Do you need to arrange for a telephone conference line (bridgeline)? Is your team in one room or located in different departments in the building? Do you have access to videoconference equipment? Do you need to think about issues that may arise because of contracts with the government or a changing regulatory environment?

Project team Perhaps the team is already predetermined, or perhaps you can lobby to draft the team yourself. Consider whom you'd like to have as your project team as well as the members' strengths and weaknesses. What influence or authority will you have over the group? Have you worked with the team before? If you haven't worked with this team before, is there anyone you know well enough to get insight into how they operate? Is there a critical person required for the project? Do you have the luxury to include cross-training in preparation for the project? Cross-training is a valuable long-term strategy to relieve the stress of having only one person in the organization with the requisite skills.

Does the identified team have the skills to successfully complete the project? If not, how will you get them trained? How many hours do you think your team will need to spend on the project? Will you need several people for a week or two? Will you need one person full-time for several months with four people working part-time? I'll discuss the project team in more detail in Chapter 4, "Drafting the Dream Team."

Budget For small projects the expectation is often that the PM will get the project done within the predefined budget established by management. The PM is responsible to try to meet that expectation *and* to let management know if that isn't possible. Consider whether you need to modify the budget or request more funding. Do you know of other projects running under budget? These projects are often measured under one cost center budget.

Project deliverables Here's where you'll consider project deliverables such as documentation, schedule, training, and new employees. Do you need to fit this into a standard production schedule? Can the project be done in phases? Does this project deliverable have to be perfect? Is there zero tolerance for customer impact? Do you need professional printing for collateral? Does the product have to be multilingual? Do you need to develop an easy-to-understand interface? You're probably thinking now, "Well, of course I want a perfect, professional easy-to-use product." But when and if the project is in trouble, can you sacrifice some of these items for one of the others? For example, in a website launch, you may be able to release the product on time and release an upgrade a month later with the improvements and still meet client expectations.

Project duration You'll go through a more formal time-estimating effort when you get to Chapter 6, "Creating the Schedule." However, during "PM reflection time," you should consider how long the project will take. Remember that the duration must also include planning, coding, internal testing, and user acceptance. Your estimate of time should include time for clients to make decisions about the project. The fiscal year of the firm can make the project more complicated from a budget viewpoint. Many firms are rigid about budgeted money being spent in the correct time frame, but projects often overlap fiscal time frames. The PM may need to spend more time with the financial stakeholders to make sure everyone understands the needs of the project. Don't let yourself get caught in the "I have plenty of time to start the project" trap. Before you know, it will be October, and you'll have to rush the project and risk not meeting the expectations.

PM commitment How many hours of your time do you think you'll need to spend on this project? Review your current commitments, and don't forget to include standing meetings, performance reviews, annual budget creation, current projects, and future commitments. Do you have enough time and energy to commit to a successful completion of this project?

Stakeholders *Stakeholders* are all the people who have either a positive or a negative impact on your project. This is a chance to list who may have a negative impact (or positive impact) on the project and why (make sure no one else sees this list!). Evaluating the stakeholder support level is a critical step, as it will help you to determine the level of communication and documentation you need. For example, if stakeholders' trust level in you is high, you need to document only the issues that further the progress of the project. If you think stakeholders don't trust you, you may need to document every discussion and decision in detail. The trust level on the team will influence how much time you'll need to schedule for documentation for the project.

Communication What are your communication preferences: e-mail, phone, pager, or paper? Identify your preferences, but understand that others on your team may have other preferences. The trick is to organize your communication so that you get the most information to the right people in the best format.

The most formal method of communication for a PM is through documentation. This seems like a small thing. But developing your documentation process is critical for your communication. What's your preference: notebooks or electronic folders? Whatever your choice, you need to start documenting and communicating right now.

Risk What risks do you know of right now? Are you working with international team members who speak different languages? Do you have potential personality conflicts on the team? Will the product delivery match the annual budget? And finally, is this a pet project of the Chief Executive Officer (CEO), and what impact will that have on the project?

Research What additional information do you need to manage this project? You'll continue to define this in more detail later, but for now, think about global issues, such as how current technology trends and the market climate for your product may affect the research you'll do throughout the project.

PM instinct What does your gut feeling tell you? Is this going to be a tough project? Or is everything in place to make this a relatively successful project? Does this project support the corporate directives, or are there people who are against this project? Is your team going to be helpful and enthusiastic, or did they have another solution in mind? What if you have a project where many of the operations people wanted another vendor? It should be clear that a close relationship with those decision makers will be critical to the success of the project. You may not be able to turn down a project that you suspect may fail, but you can use this time to identify risks and develop mitigation and contingency strategies.

Now it's time to convert your reflection time thinking into a project plan.

Introducing the Project Plan

One of the most overlooked documents for any project is the *project plan*. This is the document that describes how the project will be managed. The perfect project would allow for time for the project team to create, review, and approve the project plan. As I mentioned earlier, management often considers the project plan an extravagance for smaller projects. But as PM, you know that a project plan is the foundation of all successful projects. Without a project plan you're running the risk that you'll have to manage your project based on intuition and squeaky-wheel issue resolution.

The following are three important justifications for having a project plan:

Team communication The primary reason you'll publish your project plan is as a communication tool for the team and stakeholders. Most people expect that you'll have meetings and they will be a waste of time. Or they assume you'll have some documentation that will appear randomly throughout the project. For example, you might have a schedule that no one reads or understands. And they may assume you'll single-handedly track and resolve issues. Your project plan will document how and when you'll perform these duties and what the participant's role is in these functions. After all, many minds are better than one, and team effort will produce far better results.

Stakeholder confidence The second reason to write a project plan is to build stakeholder confidence. Having a written document to explain how you'll manage the project reinforces your commitment to the project. It will also enable the stakeholders to understand and agree to a plan that will enable them to commit support and resources. Incorporating the stakeholders in the issue resolution escalation process will reinforce their role and responsibilities on your project.

The 80-20 rule The final reason to use a project plan is to document the repeatable processes of your project. Your status reports, issue identification and resolution, status meetings, schedule status updates, and sponsor updates are all repeatable processes in a project. The goal with your project plan is to get the repeatable processes to occur without intervention 80 percent of the time. How can you do that? You have to get your team to agree to notify you of issues, status, new risks, and schedule updates. When you can accomplish this level of teamwork, then you can use your skills to negotiate and resolve the remaining 20 percent. This is a better use of your time and expertise. We've all seen managers who have to be involved with every decision. The result is that their issue resolution turnaround becomes the root cause of project schedule overruns.

TIP   For my projects, I have a standard project plan template that matches my management style, communication preferences, and corporate procedures. I merely have to tweak a few sections, and my plan is ready.

Now that you've graduated from initiating into project planning, let's discuss how to draft the project plan.

Drafting the Project Plan

Once you've contemplated the various elements of your plan during your reflection time, you're ready to actually draft the project plan. You may even find yourself using a lot of your reflection time comments in the plan itself. A team-drafted project plan will enable you to document the project management process you'll use throughout the project. This process works best if the PM has a rough draft of the document prior to meeting with the team. (I've found that project team members would rather redline documents than create them, so it's worth checking in with your team members on this point. With many small projects, time runs short, and my standard template often becomes the project plan by default.)

NOTE   You'll recall from your project management training that all process groups of project management are *iterative*. Projects don't flow from one process group to another in a clear-cut linear manner; instead, responsibilities hop back and forth through the project process groups. For example, you may need to revisit the planning phase if you're given a new set of client expectations or a larger budget in the execution phase.

Your skeleton project plan will include many of the following items, which I'll discuss throughout this book:

Goals and business objectives In this section of the project plan, you'll list the goals and business objectives and clearly define these terms. You'll include such projections as increased revenue, improved efficiency or quality, and decreased expense. Make sure the goals align with corporate objectives and are Specific, Measurable, Agreed to, Realistic, and Time-bound (SMART) goals. If you have a project that doesn't match a corporate objective, you run the risk of having the project questioned or canceled midway through the project.

Scope and scope management The *scope* of your project includes all the work required and only the work required to complete the project successfully. In this section of the project plan, you'll identify what needs to be accomplished to meet the expectations of the stakeholders. If you complete more than what's defined in the scope, then you're wasting resources. Establishing project scope and continually managing it is required for you to keep boundaries on the project.

Change management plan In this section of your project plan, you'll define how you'll identify and manage changes to scope and requirements. Change management is vital for determining which items need to be completed as part of this project. Changes can be any alteration of direction or additional requirements that are identified during the completion of the project. Usually these kinds of changes have an impact on resources, schedules, and budget and must be identified and prioritized quickly. You'll want to ask yourself, "Is there a standing committee to review, prioritize, and approve changes for the project, or is that the responsibility of the sponsor?"

Project measurements You need to define how you will measure project success. You have many ways to measure a project. I recommend following a standard set of benchmarks to measure the successful outcome of a project: time, cost, quality, scope, and customer satisfaction. Your goal should be to complete a project on the date promised, within the budget allocated, and with minimum defects that delivers a product that meets the defined requirements and satisfies customer expectations. As they say, you get what you measure. Defining the measurement criteria will define your project success.

NOTE I'll discuss goals and objectives, scope, change management, and project measurements in further detail in Chapter 2, "Defining Business Objectives, Goals, Scope, and Requirements."

Risk response plan In this portion of your project plan, you'll include a description of how you'll identify and manage risks for the project. What are project risks? They are any potential problem that can impact the outcome of a project. Identification of the risk early in a project exponentially improves the chance of success.

Stakeholder management plan Here you'll include a description of the project team members, their roles in the project, and how you will manage them. Some issues that will have an effect on the stakeholder management plan include whether you work in a *matrixed organization*, where people are temporarily assigned to a project, and whether the *functional managers*, the people who are the formal supervisors of your team members, are in favor of the project. Functional managers are the managers your team members report to for raises and non-project-related direction.

Communication plan We all know that a PM will spend up to 90 percent of her time communicating to the stakeholders about the project, so the communications plan is the most critical part of the project plan. One of the first communications you need to have with your team is the description of how you'll distribute project information. Will you communicate with the team, stakeholders, and the sponsor in a formal or informal manner? Will you do this via e-mail or phone? How will you escalate issues? How will you get quick resolution of issues?

Issue management plan What is an *issue*? It can be a question, a problem, a potential risk, or a to-do. Often issues are too small an item to be tracked on a schedule. In the issues management plan, you'll describe how you'll track, manage, and closeout these kinds of concerns. Issues need to be raised, assigned, and closed out continually during the project. Make sure your issue management plan also includes a process to have closed issues tested during the quality-testing portion of your project.

NOTE   I'll discuss the stakeholder management plan, the communication plan, and the issues management plan in more detail in Chapter 4.

Budget estimates In the budget estimates portion of the project plan, you'll include a description of how you'll review and validate the budget for the project. The budget is usually one of the main project measurement criteria for any project. I'll discuss project budgets in more detail in Chapter 5, "Finalizing Estimates and Budgets."

Schedule and milestones Your project plan will also include a description of how you'll distribute and communicate the schedule, critical path, milestones, and their status through the schedule and milestones section. Meeting your due date is the second most used criteria for project success. Management likes this measurement because it's easy to determine whether the project is on track and whether you can meet your date. In Chapter 6, "Creating the Schedule," I'll discuss scheduling and milestones further.

Quality management plan The quality management plan will include a description of how you plan to manage quality for the project. This is where you'll incorporate the corporate quality polices and procedures into your project, including processes for benchmarking, testing, and auditing. I'll review quality methods in Chapter 7, "Defining the Quality Plan."

Procurement management plan Procurement management includes contract administration and equipment/service purchasing. Both of these functions can have long lead times, which reinforces the need to define your plan and your procurement deliverables early in the project. Dragging your feet to initiate a requisition or meet with your legal team could make the difference in whether you'll meet your project date. In Chapter 8, "Defining the Procurement Management Plan," I'll review strategies to identify, schedule, and manage procurement deliverables.

Approvals and project kickoff Obtaining project plan approvals are necessary to finalize the scope, commit resources, and get buy-in for the project. Once those approvals are obtained, you're ready for the team kickoff to begin work on the project. In Chapter 9, "Revealing the Plan," we'll discuss strategies and techniques for the project kickoff.

I recommend you develop a standard project plan template that you're familiar with, which you can continue to use when you're assigned new projects. Throughout our continued discussions of the intricacies and importance of properly planning a project, I'll discuss the elements of the project plan. Before I go into a deeper discussion of project objective and scope, I'll cover how project initiating and the PM reflection fit into the greater scheme of project management.

PROJECT LIFE CYCLE VS. PRODUCT LIFE CYCLE

After passing the Project Management Professional (PMP) exam, I was determined and enthusiastic to incorporate what I learned into my project processes. I also have a penchant to combine processes where possible. So I tried to map the product life-cycle documents into the project life cycle. I spent hours trying to figure out where the design documents fit into the planning process group. I expressed my frustration during lunch with my fellow PMs.

The result was one of the epiphanies of my PM career. A wise mentor explained the difference between a *project life cycle* and a *product life cycle* and why you need both. The product life cycle is how you do the work. This will include documenting your analysis, coding, printing, building, testing, and implementing. The project life cycle is the life cycle of the project, which includes the five process groups of a project. The project life cycle includes how you plan and manage the project, as well as the project reviews and closeout. The crossover emphasis for this book is that you document your plan for how you'll manage how the team performs the work per the product life cycle.

Case Study

Patricia is the new engineering manager for Volte Corporation, a company that provides software and hardware solutions for a patented voice-recognition product. Her primary responsibility is to manage five software and five hardware engineers. She is known for her organizational skills and "get it done" attitude. One morning on the way to get coffee she meets up with Laurie, her boss's boss. The two discuss a potential client implementation that has an expected due date eight months from today. Laurie asks if Patricia has time to look at the draft of the SOW and provide her with feedback by the end of the day.

Patricia refreshes her coffee while thinking about the opportunity. Back at the office, she calls her boss, Bob, to ask about the project and the SOW review she was just asked to provide.

Bob says, "Oh yeah, we were discussing this in last week's department meeting, and your name came up as someone who could handle the conversion. We need this client implementation as a strategic hook into the market. I think you'd do a great job. I know your schedule is pretty tight right now, but I think this would be a great addition to your resume.

"There are a couple of things I think you should know about the project. First of all, a similar project was done two years ago with moderate success. As I recall, the client was Brown Enterprises. The PM who was in charge of that project left the company shortly after the project's completion. I'm sure there's documentation, somewhere. Maybe you could talk to Jeff in Document Control to find out where to start looking.

"The company you'll be converting this time around is a previous client who left our services because of conflicts with our old management team and a very bad conversion of their top customers. In fact, several of their own customers left them because of that conversion. Some of the original Brown Enterprises management team is still with Brown Enterprises and will be working with you on this project. I don't think they have confidence in our ability to pull this off.

"Sorry I hadn't gotten around to talking to you about it. Do you think you could squeeze it into you commitments?"

Patricia agrees to think about it and get back to him at the end of the day with her answer. She walks back to her office, looks at her schedule, and sees that she has couple of hours to review the project. She finds a quiet location and pulls out her standard project reflection questions. She reviews and completes the following as her preliminary project review:

Process history Yes. Volte Corporation does have a process to follow for this project but only for projects greater than 5000 hours. Work orders initiate internal work, and SOWs are used for initiating external projects. I need to find and collect the project documentation for the previous conversion implementation.

Project sponsor Yes. The sponsor for this project will be Laurie. She is well connected and well respected. This project will be a foundation to grow the market share of the company, which is one of the top three corporate goals, so this will be an incentive for Laurie to be committed to the success of the project. I've worked with her before, and we communicate easily.

Resources I have the current software, a workspace, and a project team available. I need hardware for implementation.

Project team Jay and Mike: two software engineers. Christina, John, and Jodi: three hardware engineers. Also needed: standing legal, purchasing, technical writing, and publishing members.

Budget No. This project will be similar to the previous project. I'll need to find last project costs as a place to start. I will still need an itemized budget for this project with all the resources/contractors/materials listed.

Expectations Declared: Client expects eight-month schedule. Client expects zero client impact as a result of the conversion.

Undeclared: I need to talk to the sales person to identify any other promises for this contract.

Project duration Eight-month implementation and conversion turn-around. Hardware has eight-week turnaround, once ordered. Training needs to be held one week before launch. New contracts typically take twelve weeks to execute.

PM commitment I currently have six hours of standing meetings per week. Each meeting requires thirty minutes prep time, for a total of nine hours. I am averaging eight to twelve hours per week for project management for two other projects over the next eight weeks. This project will require at least eight hours per week for the first several weeks. That leaves about five hours per week to manage my team.

Stakeholders The stakeholders for this project include the sponsor, the project team, the attorneys, purchasing, all the functional managers, and the client. The client has worked with the previous vendor for 10 years. The operations manager wanted to contract with the other vendor and is sure you can't perform or convert. I need to build a strategy to improve trust with the client.

Communication The company has a standard format for collecting the project documents in folders on the Local Area Network (LAN). My preference for communications is e-mail; however, Laurie prefers phone and voicemail. The client team will include members across several states in several time zones. I'll need to make sure I have access to a telephone conference line for meetings and issue resolution.

Risk Depending on the kickoff, this project may be implemented in December. I need to get everyone's vacations schedules. I also need to get reservations early for the implementation team to travel to the client's site.

Research Is there a better technology that should be used for this conversion that wasn't used in the last conversion? Is there technology that would make implementation and configuration quicker and cheaper? I need to look into this.

PM instinct The sponsor, Laurie, will be helpful. I know most of the team and have the authority to select the rest of the team. This project has enough priority and visibility to be able to get additional resources as necessary. The vendor trust issue will be an obstacle. I'll need to work on the relationship with the client and make sure I have good escalation procedures. Maybe we could have the project kick off on-site with the client. I need to make sure I order the hardware early to avoid the end-of-the-year rush. My time commitments are pretty tight for the next few weeks. But this project will be worth my time and efforts.

After Patricia reflects on her initial project review, she decides she is up for the challenge. She sends an e-mail to Bob and Laurie to let them know she can work this into her schedule. She begins reviewing the statement of work and schedules a time to go over those comments with Laurie the next morning.

CHAPTER 2

Defining Project Objectives, Goals, Scope, and Requirements

Now that you've initiated the project, the next step is to define the project objectives, scope, goals, and requirements for the project. Good project definition starts with the objectives of the project and ends with approved detailed requirements. Project objectives, goals, scope, and requirements describe the project in ever-increasing detail. But the terms overlap, and you may find it difficult to decide where you should place your statements in your project plan. For instance, is "comply with ISO 9000 standards" an objective, a goal, or a part of your scope statement? Unless you know the proper definitions for each, you may not know which it is, and if you don't know, you can mislead your team in the process.

Project objectives are the descriptions that support corporate direction, such as increased revenue and decreased expenses, and are usually realized at a future time. *Goals* are the finish-line measurements for the project that determine project success. *Scope* is the boundary of the project and is the high-level description of stakeholder expectations. And, finally, the *requirements* define the characteristics of the deliverables. Together these terms provide direction for a project team to successfully meet the stakeholder expectations.

In this chapter, I'll discuss project objectives, goals, scope, and requirements in further detail, so you can understand their distinguishing features and communicate their purpose to your project teams properly.

Setting Project Objectives and Goals

Project objectives and goals are the main point at which the project success will be measured. They're usually the first items used to justify doing the project and the foundation for all descriptions of the project. Often project objectives and goals are identified by the project sponsor or other high-level stakeholders and are presented to the PM.

The pyramid in Figure 2.1 shows the hierarchy of the project descriptions. The foundation of the pyramid are the project objectives of the organization, which are a few statements that tie the project purpose to the project objectives. Next are the project goals, which are the finish-line measurements for this project that build on the project objectives. Next are the project scope statements that define the boundaries of the project and determine the project deliverables. And at the top of the pyramid are the requirements, which detail the characteristics of the deliverables defined in the scope. While each layer is built on the concepts of the previous layer, each higher layer should also have more detail and volume than the lower layer.

FIGURE 2.1: Pyramid of project objectives, goals, scope, and requirements

WHAT'S IN A NAME?

You wouldn't think it'd be that important, but the name or title you give a project can cause repercussions later in a project life cycle. Take, for instance, a situation I recently encountered. I was given a list of projects to prioritize. Six of the twenty-five projects were titled "Web Implementation." I had no way to differentiate one project from the next other than the name of the PM. I couldn't prioritize the projects because the titles weren't descriptive enough for me to know what they involved. No one did this on purpose to confuse management. But in this case, each PM had only one web implementation to manage, so the brief title was descriptive enough for them and their team. When you select a title of your project, it should be long enough that it differentiates similar projects but short enough that you won't mind typing it over and over and over again. You could change Web Implementation to Brown Ent. Web Implementation or Brown Ent. Web Imp 2005.

Project Objectives

It's a PM's job to make certain project goals line up with the business objectives of the organization. Project objectives define the big picture, the expected impact of the project on the business, and are the reasons for doing the project in the first place. Project objectives are often given to the PM during the project assignment. Let's say the purpose of a new project is to create a new bubble-making toy. This project was probably identified during an annual planning process to support the business objectives to increase revenue and to expand the patent portfolio. The idea appeared to have merit, and senior management decided to pursue the project.

It's sometimes difficult to ensure that the project objectives align with the business objectives. Often smaller projects have rather obscure connections with the business goals and objectives. This is where your knowledge of the organization will come in handy. You may be able to use multiple projects in conjunction to satisfy one project objective. For example, your project may improve a maintenance process that doesn't directly support any business objectives. However, one of the business objectives is to increase sales to new clients. The cumulative effect is that if you don't improve the maintenance process, the system won't be available for new clients to use; thus, sales can't be fulfilled to new clients.

Business Justification

The *business justification* is the reason the business took on the project . The cost estimate here will be a rather rough estimate, usually based on experience, which is used to see if the project is even worth doing. The sponsor should supply the benefit portion of the business justification. The executive managers will use these cost-benefit figures to evaluate all projects, prioritize all acceptable projects, and decide which projects to do.

Business justifications tend to be strictly the numbers end of the evaluation and may not take into account any intangible benefits that may come from doing the project. If you're lucky, you'll have a sponsor who includes quantified intangible benefits in the business justification. The bubble-making project justification might include $1 million for research and development; $500,000 for miscellaneous expenses; and $2 million in revenues for the first year. The net earnings are projected to be $500,000. This project will then be placed in the list of other potential projects and prioritized by corporate benefit. Intangible benefits may be used as tiebreakers. For example, increased company knowledge about bubble technology may place the company in a stronger competitive position that outweighs the intangible benefits of another project with the same net earnings.

Team Goals

Team goals are the results team members expect to achieve by finishing this project. As you'd expect, these goals are best if they're defined by the project team. Team goals include items such as the increased knowledge of a technology, improved knowledge of other departments, or enhanced presentation skills. These goals appear in the individual performance reviews under employee development. These goals are expectations that each team member is measured on and goals that are often missed during the creation of the project plan.

Before you can establish the team or project goals, you need to find out how the team's functional departments measure the team member's performance; otherwise, you may unknowingly be creating conflict in your team. If one of the requirements of your project is to clean inactive customers off of the database, and some of your team is rewarded by the number of customers they maintain on the database, you may get passive resistance for aggressively removing customers. Team members will be even more reluctant if bonuses are tied to these goals. If you don't identify this during the project goal setting, everyone will be surprised at the conclusion of the project. Either the project will meet its goals, with many of the team being unhappy because they don't get their bonuses, or you don't meet the project goals and some of the team is rewarded by their functional department.

Defining Project Goals

The next level of detail for the project is the project goals. *Project goals* are the ends or final purposes of the project. Think of these as the project measurements as you cross the project finish line. They're the objective measurement that determines the success of the project. Sometimes the sponsor gives the team their goals, and sometimes the team can set the project goals. A word of advice: don't select too many goals to measure, as the team will get confused and not be able to focus on anything. I suggest you select no more than six project goals. I'm sure you've been on teams that have identified six project objectives, ten team goals, and twelve project goals. During the project they all begin to merge, overlap, and contradict one another. Then when you start to track the goals, you find the team is spending so much time on learning the technology to complete the team goal that the schedule date for the project goal is at risk.

SMART Goals

All project goals must follow the SMART criteria. I am sure you're familiar with the term, but the following is a brief refresher of the acronym:

Specific Your goal statements should be clear and concise rather than broad and vague. For example, "Deliver version 6.2 of widget product," rather than "Deliver next phase."

Measurable Your goal should have an easy-to-obtain measure to verify that you did or didn't meet the goal. This usually takes the format of a number or date. If you use a formula, keep it simple, or you'll be explaining and defending it ad nauseam.

Agreed to Your goal must have enough detail that the team can agree on whether they met the goal. If you don't get agreement on the goal, you'll most certainly not get agreement on the deliverable.

Realistic Your goal must be able to be done within reasonable limits. For example, the date must be achievable, and the deliverable must be doable. Unrealistic goals create unrealistic stakeholder expectations that may result in apathetic team attitudes. After all, why expend the time and energy on a project you know can't meet the goals?

Time-bound Your goal must have a beginning and end date, not an open-ended duration. If you can't determine an end date, you probably have an operations process rather than a project.

PICK YOUR GOALS CAREFULLY

Remember, you get what you measure, so think through your measurement. I knew a company that had the business objective to lower lost time injury rate. The Occupational Safety and Health Administration (OSHA) definition of Lost Time Injury (LTI) was measured by an employee missing a full shift because of an injury at work. At the end of the year, voila! The LTI rate was indeed lower. However, a closer look at the numbers showed that the number of employees who were injured was actually higher. How did the LTI number go down? The managers made sure the employees were not off work for eight hours. Some managers even drove injured employees to work and let them sleep on a cot in the corner. The corporation got what it asked for but didn't get what they wanted.

Measuring Your Goals

The *triple constraint* is a widely used set of project goals: time, cost and quality. Usually the triple constraint is used company-wide, as it can be used to compare results of dissimilar projects.

The triple constraint, illustrated in Figure 2.2, is often shown as a triangle to demonstrate how all three are tightly bound. If you want high quality, it will cost you time and dollars. If you want it quicker, that will also cost you more, and you risk lowering quality. If you want it cheap, it may take longer, and the quality is again at risk.

Over time, PMs have commonly included two additional measurements of project goals: scope and client satisfaction. These ensure that the project delivers the product as defined by the scope statements and that there's an effort to meet client expectations. Otherwise, it's fairly easy to deliver something that works perfectly, meets the budget and schedule, but doesn't do anything the client expected.

FIGURE 2.2: The triple constraint

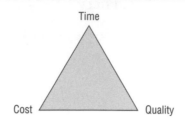

The tricky part with using quality, scope, and client satisfaction as project goals is that the project team will have to define what will be used to measure these goals. These can all be tough items to measure and will most likely be a source of team debate. For example, how do you know that the stakeholders are pleased with the project deliverables? Do they attend meetings with smiley happy faces, or do they sign off on the project? Neither may be clear indicators that the project met the stakeholders' expectations. Why? Because the happy faces may be that they enjoy attending team meetings because they like interacting with the team. The subsequent sign-off may mean that they're eager to end the relationship with the team. Briefly, let's review the most common five goals:

Time Time can be measured in duration, hour estimates, or dates.

Cost The cost of the project is the budget of the project. This will include any approved increases resulting from scope changes.

Quality The team will have to determine the quality measurement of the project. Quality can be measured by defects, bugs, or rejected product.

Scope This goal is the measurement of whether the project delivered what was expected. To help define the scope goal, you may want to refer to the change management process. The team may use the number of approved change notices or the number of requirements added after the baseline approval.

Client satisfaction Project success is measured primarily by meeting stakeholder expectations. This is a slippery goal, as you can meet the time, cost, quality, and scope goals and still not satisfy the client. The team will have to define how to measure this goal. Surveys or interviews are often the method used to collect this data.

NOTE   Keep the goals on everyone's radars by posting them in either the physical or virtual project team room or by reporting on the status weekly.

GOAL OVERLOAD

Have you ever worked with a company that requested you develop personal goals to support the business objectives, behavior/value goals, and department goals? This would all be great if the personal goals were built upon the behavior goals, which were built upon department goals, which were built on the business objectives. In many cases, the goals aren't in sync but rather are independent, nonrelated goals. I worked with a company, and we were required to come up with 18 independent goals. At the end of the year the employees used their creative-writing skills to generate the story about how they met their goals.

Critical Success Factors

Critical success factors are what you absolutely positively must have in place for the project to be successful. This is another list you need to keep to a minimum to manage effectively. Make sure you have these items identified in your risk plan, including the corresponding mitigation strategies. As you're creating the list of critical success factors, you may think you're repeating yourself because the same list may also appear in the project plan as assumptions and goals. As an example, requiring a project sponsor, having realistic defined expectations, or having no new legislation impact the product, are all statements that can show up under several sections of the project plan. If an item keeps showing up in different sections as you draft your plan, make sure you keep it on your radar throughout the project, as it may be the item that needs the most care. In the bubble-toy project, a critical success factor may be that the patent investigation doesn't show potential patent infringements.

Assumptions

We all know what *assume* means. However, to accurately define a project it's imperative that the PM lists the *assumptions*. Assumptions are things that are taken for granted, and consequently they aren't easy to gather. Why spend the time to collect assumptions? You should do this to identify potential disconnects by the stakeholders. You'll find that these disconnects generally fall into two categories: definitions and understanding.

Different groups have different interpretations for the same term. If the team has a definition disconnect early in the project, everyone is going to be surprised by the final product. A simple example is that programmers define user-friendly screens as they comply with current web standards. On the other hand, user-friendly screens to a customer service representative include features that a non–web user can intuitively follow.

The second cause for many disconnects is the level of understanding by the stakeholders. A stakeholder may not know they don't know, so they can't ask the clarifying question. As the PM, you'll need to try to think like all the stakeholders to ask as many questions as you can. For example, if you're running the project to rewrite a human resource system, you need to ask the detailed questions about converting current human resource records, data entry, and record retention.

Stakeholders may have vastly different responsibilities, such as operations, maintenance, and engineering, with no understanding of each other's perspective. The disconnect happens here because one group assumes the other group understands the impact of a joint decision. For example, in building a garage, the project team is notified that the concrete vendor is going to be delayed for a week. The construction team knows this means the entire project has now slipped a week because the concrete must be poured prior to building the garage. But the homeowner may think it's just another piece of the project that can be worked around that will not impact the end date.

NOTE Assumptions are often recording the obvious, because the obvious isn't always readily apparent to all stakeholders.

The following are some assumptions that the PM should understand. This isn't an exhaustive list but rather a list of items that can be "gotchas":

Priority Know where your project stands in the priority line. Otherwise you'll be surprised when your resources are pulled from your project to support another project with higher priority. Also, you'll need to monitor the progress of higher priority projects so that you can be ready to make adjustments in your project in case you need to support other teams.

Regulatory environment The PM needs to know the regulatory environment in which they're working. Do you work for a company that requires Federal Drug Administration (FDA) approval for their products? Or does your company have to work with the Environmental Protection Agency (EPA) or OSHA guidelines? Not only do you need to be aware of the current regulations but also the company policies used to meet those regulations. Depending on your industry, you need to be aware of pending regulations or legislation that may impact your project.

Team stability Since most company reorganizations are "hush-hush" until the ax falls, you have to assume that no company reorganizations will impact the resources of the project. You may be thinking, "Well, of course reorganizations would impact the project, why should I write down this obvious assumption?" But your sponsor may be aware of a pending reorganization and hadn't thought about how that could impact this project. You're stating the obvious in order to remind them that you may need to regroup if this comes to pass.

Team scope You must assume that all stakeholders agree to the project scope, goals, charter, and project plan. Write this down, because you'll be surprised at the number of times that someone comes in at the end of the project with several additional requirements they knew were necessary but "forgot" to share. For the bubble-toy project, someone may have forgotten to disclose that the current bubble formula patent has a pending infringement claim. This impacts the scope of the project, as one of the assumptions may be that you're going to use the company's current bubble formula.

Other pressures on the project This is where you identify the miscellaneous pressures on the project. Does the project have critical timing assumptions, such as the product must be ready for Christmas sales? Or is this the CEO's pet project? I didn't believe this was possible, but I worked on a project that the CEO thought was a great idea. We delivered the product as required, but no one bought it. This was a difficult project to finish because the entire team knew instinctively it wouldn't fly, but the CEO held firm on his decision. We met the project goals, but the project objectives never came to fruition.

The last thing that you need to do before you delineate scope is to validate the project assumptions. Assumptions are often collected during a brainstorming session. One of the brainstorming rules is that you gather all statements and validate them later. If you do not validate the assumptions, you may find errors during the project and not have sufficient time to respond effectively. For example, you may assume that the project is the number one priority. This assumption impacts the ability to keep skilled resources working on the project. Let's say the PM obtains a copy of the annual budget to validate the assumption and they find that the project is a high priority but not the top priority. The project team can adjust the assumption statement and develop risk management plans before another project takes critical project resources.

Delineating Scope

Once you have defined the project objectives and goals, it is time to delineate the project scope. *Scope* defines the project by describing the limits of activities and deliverables. This section of the project plan is where you delineate what you'll be providing and what your team will be doing. The project scope and subsequent deliverables will be the basis for your requirements, schedules, and budgets.

The sponsor and stakeholders create the *scope statements*, which are the project boundaries. Refer to Appendix B for a Project Scope Statement template. These boundaries need to be clear enough to be the basis of all project decisions and be what you'll use to manage the project and its deliverables. I've seen projects that have a one-line scope statement, but that's never enough information to completely describe the project. You need to have enough description of the scope so you can tell whether something is within the scope of this project or whether you need to put it on the future phase list.

Once you have the initial set of scope statements, it's helpful to run this by the team to make sure you haven't missed anything. The team scope review meeting will not only improve the completeness of the project scope but also validate that the team understands the project.

It's the PM's responsibility to make sure you don't *gold plate* the deliverables. What's gold plating? It's the process whereby you deliver more than what's needed to have a successful product. There's continual pressure to unintentionally gold plate a deliverable to keep the stakeholders happy. Gold plating leads to scope creep, which may make it difficult or impossible to reach your project goals.

Scope creep. The term conjures visions of zombies slowly creeping out of their graves, slowly, almost imperceptibly, slithering forward along the ground beneath the field of vision of its victim, until quite unexpectedly it grabs its victim. That is exactly what scope creep does to a PM. Little tasks are added to the scope of the project, almost imperceptibly, until quite unexpectedly you find your delivery date has slipped.

As the PM, you don't intentionally let the scope creep. You may have an opportunity to stop it, or you may not see it happening. For example, your project is to revise the website to match the new-and-improved trade marking for the company. While the web designers are revising the trademarks and colors on the screen, one of the stakeholders points out that they've been collecting criticisms about the site since it was launched two years ago. Do you add the changes? You probably don't, because it's clear that the request is out of scope. But what about if the project scope allows for the button color changes to match the look and feel of the home page of the current site? While changing the buttons, you're asked to change the verbiage on the buttons to be more user-friendly and descriptive. This seems like a trivial change. So you let it in. Then the button language changes take longer than expected, and the next thing you know you've added 40 hours to the project. Was the language change in scope? It's easy to say "no" to this decision in hindsight, as it's out of scope. Both of these decisions aren't so easy while you're managing the project.

WHAT'S NOT IN SCOPE?

If you're having a tough time trying to identify what's in scope, then try the reverse approach. Define what's *not* in scope. Like in art, this will put the boundaries around the project, and then you add the detail of what's left. For example, you're *not* revising the base product, you're *not* including international addresses, and you're *not* delivering context-sensitive help screens. What's left? A website with no screen flow changes and U.S. addresses with the current help functionality.

This is also a useful technique to collect requirements for future projects or phases. You can include all those items that come up during the project that are defined as out of scope. You'll have given yourself a head start on scope and requirements for the next release and phase of the product.

Baseline Deliverables List

Define the baseline *deliverables*. I intentionally use the term *baseline*, as you'll often identify additional deliverables as you work through the project.

Deliverables can easily become your first list of *milestones*, as deliverables are easy to identify as complete. Most people think the product is *the* deliverable. But you may also have some other features that will be delivered as part of the project. Some typical things you may want to include in the deliverables list are new procedures, product documentation, client training, new forms, marketing collateral, and interim versions of any major deliverable (prototypes, pilot versions, and so on). For the bubble-toy example, in addition to the actual toy, you'll need advertising, a manufacturing plan, a distribution strategy, approved trademarks, and patent applications.

NOTE   You need to clearly define the acceptance criteria of each deliverable because the word *complete* to one person may be incomplete to another.

Requirements

A PM will spend a significant part of their time collecting and managing requirements. And yet, at the end of a project, if anything has gone awry, the root cause is almost always that there wasn't enough time spent on requirements. Since I'm talking about smaller projects, there's usually little time between project initiation and product launch. The parties usually have little time to let the ideas percolate to collect all the requisite requirements. The following ideas should help remedy those problems.

Requirements Collection

Requirements aren't deliverables but characteristics that allow you to validate that the deliverables meet the needs of the stakeholders. The bubble toy is the deliverable, and the requirements include that it's made of colorful plastic, that there are no small detachable parts, and that the toy is dishwasher safe, all of which are characteristics of the toy. It's the responsibility of the stakeholders to create requirements, and it's the PM's job is to facilitate the collection of these requirements.

RIDICULOUS BRAINSTORMING SUGGESTIONS

Brainstorming rules encourage everyone to state everything that comes to mind, regardless of how ridiculous the idea appears. Some of the best solutions will be stimulated by the ridiculous idea. I was part of a brainstorming session on reducing injuries. One of the workers joked that it must be the noise and vibration of the tools that was causing injuries. Initially, everyone thought that was ridiculous. However, we checked with an occupational therapist who explained segmental vibration, which can cause repetitive injuries to hands, wrists, and elbows. We purchased newer tools that did not vibrate as much, thus reducing the injuries. A joke lead to the eventual solution.

This is where you may want to use the sticky-note brainstorming process. Give everyone a pad of sticky notes, and have them write requirements on the pad, one requirement per page. Then, each person presents their collection of requirements. The presentation of ideas often stimulates ideas of other team members. Another advantage to the sticky-note process is that as you redefine the categories of the requirements, you can easily move them around on the wall. Pulling them off the wall and keeping them intact is another story. You may want to use a piece of butcher paper as the backdrop for your requirement collage.

Reason for Requirements

Requirements are also helpful to remind stakeholders of the agreed-upon project. The further you get from the kickoff meetings, the more creative their memories become. Imagine if at the last hour one of the stakeholders remembers that you promised to have the manuals spiral bound, not stapled. More than likely this wasn't identified as a requirement for the manuals in the meeting. This falls into one of those understanding disconnects because the stakeholder thought everyone knew it was the company standard to spiral bind books, and no one else in the room had ever published a company manual.

Your quality group or test group will appreciate detailed requirements, as they can easily roll into test plans. Requirements that start with a phrases such as "The product shall..." are easily reusable and can be converted to pass or fail product tests.

As hard as you work to collect all the requirements, inevitably a stakeholder will bring up items that weren't previously identified "that we absolutely need to launch the product." When this happens, you flash back to the requirements-gathering meetings. You remember all the people in the room, you recall the requirements discussion, you know the stakeholders approved the plan, and yet here is another surprise. What happened? I call this the *awakening* portion of the project, where the stakeholders finally become mentally engaged in the project and have really begun to think through the scope of the project. I don't think most people do this intentionally. Somehow they think there would be more time before the product is launched to think through the details. They thought the project would never really come to fruition. Either way, you need to try to push these requirements to the next portion of the project. If the item must be done now, follow the change notice process to roll it into this phase. Make sure you clearly identify the impact to the project; otherwise, as the PM, you'll take the hit.

Approval for Scope

Who should approve the scope? First and foremost, the sponsor should. You need their approval of the scope for buy-in and commitment to the project. You also need to make sure you're all on the same page so that you have their support in the decisions you make during the management of the project.

More and more companies are following quality processes, which I'll discuss in more detail in Chapter 7, "Defining the Quality Plan." Every one of these processes has an auditing feature, which emphasizes formal approvals as a check and balance throughout the project. This is a logical place in the project planning process to obtain approvals. The last reason to have approval at this point in the project is to be able to show the approved direction of the project. This not only helps the PM manage the project but also lets the team members know the "whats" and "whys" of the project.

Approvals can either be by e-mail or with a signature. Make sure you keep approvals with the project documentation so that you can produce approvals during any potential audit.

One last note: verbal approvals will always get you in trouble. It's tough enough to manage a project with formal approvals. If you choose to manage projects with verbal direction, you also choose to be responsible for the consequences of that action. The PM will be held responsible for the miscommunications with regard to the product deliverables.

Scope Management Plan

Typically, the project objectives will stay relatively steady during the course of the project. Most companies don't drastically change their business objectives from year to year much less during the short duration of a project. But the goals, scope, assumptions, and requirements will most likely change throughout the project. I know all project managers wish that once they have project plan approval that the requirements never change. If we were all omniscient like Jean-Luc Picard, that might be possible. But we are not all Starfleet captains, we are PMs who have our memories and thoughts triggered as we move through the project. Some of the issues raised during the course of the project will just clarify questions. But some of the issues will result in scope changes that impact the schedule, cost, and resources. The PM is responsible for identifying the impact and managing these changes.

Refer to the *Project Manager's Spotlight on Change Management* book for methodologies and additional tricks to keep the scope on track. Document your scope management process, and include it in the project plan. You'll need to follow a disciplined approach to encourage the stakeholders to formally submit the changes as they're identified throughout the project. It's worthwhile to take some time to define the scope management plan, as it's one of the areas that may remain consistent from project to project. See Appendix B for a template to help you create your project scope statement.

NOTE   Make sure you revise goals, scope documentation, and requirements as changes are approved for the project.

In closing, remember that the project objectives, goals, scope, and requirements build and support each other. Each contributes to the definitions of the project and the deliverables.

NOTE   For more information about keeping the scope on track, see Claudia Baca's *Project Manager's Spotlight on Change Management* (Sybex, 2005).

Case Study

The PM, Patricia, pulled up her template for the scope statement and began to collect data from the previous similar conversion. Patricia met with Jeff, and they found some of the old project documentation, meager as it was. All that was left was the contract, schedule, and several weekly reports. She was able to identify the original budget and resource estimates from the weekly reports. Patricia validated that the implementation and conversion can be done in eight months with similar requirements. The previous contract can be used as the first draft of the contract between Volte Corporation and Brown Enterprises.

Patricia began to interview people to collect information about the current project. Her first interview was with the salesman, Troy. He confirmed that there's reluctance by several members of Brown Enterprises to convert to Volte. Troy said he shared with Brown Enterprises management that he has a new management team that has perfected the conversion process. However, Troy casually mentioned he promised that the voice-recognition product would also recognize Spanish. As this isn't a current feature of the product, Patricia will have to investigate where the code is in the development cycle. Troy also promised the product would be able to support the functionality to collect five random questions for voice matching within a year. Patricia flinched at that point, knowing that the multi-question technology hasn't been prioritized to be included in next year's development plan.

Next Patricia met with Laurie to draft the project objectives and scope. Laurie pulled the annual company business objectives from her desk drawer. They discussed and drafted the project and team goals. Laurie reviewed the current corporate plan, which included goals on supporting values, project objectives, and personal development. Patricia was adamant they keep the list to a small number of goals for the project so that she could keep the team focused on a few SMART goals.

Patricia used the old weekly reports to start the assumption and deliverables list. The rest of the team contributed to the scope, assumptions, deliverables, and requirements. Laurie reviewed and approved the project plan scope descriptions. The following sections review some of the key parts of the project plan.

Project Objectives

The project objectives that Patricia is focusing on are to increase market penetration by adding one of the top five users, to improve standard processes for configuration and conversion, and to increase revenue with the new end users.

Goals

Patricia has developed the standard goals into SMART goals for her project. They are as follows:

Cost The project estimate is $450,000 billable to the client within 30 days of projection completion.

Schedule The project will be completed within eight months beginning with the executed contract and ending with client acceptance.

Quality The conversion will be completed with fewer than 15 bug reports from the quality assurance testing process.

Scope There will be no more than three change notices identified and approved during the duration of the project.

Customer satisfaction Customer satisfaction will be defined as zero customer impacts for conversion, measured at the end with a project survey sent to 10 percent of the converted customers selected randomly.

Scope

The high-level boundaries for the project are to convert approximately 10,000 customers to the new voice-recognition hardware for Brown Enterprises in eight months, to configure hardware to support implementation, to add Spanish to the voice-recognition software, to print branded user guides and collateral, and to have an executed contract with Brown Enterprises prior to customer conversion.

Not in Scope

Patricia has identified the following features as not part of the scope of this phase of the project: the ability to collect five questions for random matching, no new customers, no changes to current product flow, and no changes to language on user guides or marketing collateral.

Deliverables

The primary deliverable for the project is the configuration of hardware and conversion of 10,000 customers for Brown Enterprises. In addition, the product must have Spanish as part of the recognition product. This conversion project is expected to be the first of many conversions. So an added expectation is that there will be significant process improvements for configuration and conversion.

Requirements

Patricia held two meetings with the stakeholders and collected a rather extensive list of requirements that defines the characteristics of all the project deliverables. The list has been shared with the project team and SMEs to ensure that the answers to all their questions have been given in the requirements. In addition, the list has been sent to the quality department for review.

Assumptions

Patricia uncovered several assumptions during the scope and requirements collections meetings. First, the project can't begin using resources until the contract is executed. Second, the project will follow current corporate QA and scope change management procedures.

The team is aware of two other projects that have a higher priority than this project. No team members are working on either of these projects. However, Jay is considered the corporate subject matter expert for one of the projects and may be called upon for some support.

No new legislation/regulation will impact the project. In addition, no company restructurings have been identified at this time. This means that there's no expected team turnover once the project has begun.

Patricia is confident that the identified stakeholders will agree to project goals, scope, requirements, and the project plan. However, she plans to review the requirements at several intervals during the projects to encourage uncovering "unknown" requirements.

CHAPTER 3

Defining Your Risk Management Plan

*R*isk management has become a sophisticated science that has its roots in probability theory. Look at the insurance industry and how it uses actuarial tables to measure and evaluate risk. These are risk tables that determine your insurance premiums. Actuaries are the kings of risk management and have developed an entire career of risk analysis. Project management has also developed a substantial disciplined approach to identifying and analyzing risks in projects. The problem is that the process may be a bit more rigorous than is needed for your project. This chapter describes a slimmed-down version that will be more useful for smaller projects.

We will identify the risks of the project using the scope statements that were identified in Chapter 2 and previous similar project experience. Project risk identification is the next level of detail required prior to creating the project budget and schedules (reviewed in Chapter 5, "Estimates and Budgets," and Chapter 6, "Creating the Schedule"). This chapter will begin by defining the method for writing the risk management plan.

NOTE   For detailed information on how to identify and manage project risks, refer to Kim Heldman's *Project Manager's Spotlight on Risk Management* (Harbor Light Press, 2005).

Planning for Risk Management

The beginning of the risk management process is the risk management plan. Risk management has two parts: risk management planning and risk response planning. *Risk management planning* is what an organization does to formalize its risk management process. It's the company's agreed-upon risk process. *Risk response planning* is what the PM and the project team create to respond to and manage identified risks on the project. I'll discuss risk response planning later in this chapter in the section, "Creating a Risk Response Plan."

Defining Your Risk Management Plan

Why do you need to have a risk management plan? Experience has shown us we need to aggressively identify and address risks early in the planning phase of the project to avoid impact to the project. Taking a proactive approach to risks gives your team more time to develop better options to deal with risks. Waiting to react to risks limits your ability to create flexible options. The project sponsor and critical stakeholders need to be involved in the creation of the risk management plan, as they're more likely to be familiar with the company-defined process. If your company has yet to define a risk management process, your team can demonstrate the value of risk management.

Creating Your Risk Management Plan

The project plan includes the risk management plan, which can easily be reused from project to project within the same company. The following are sections that should be included in the risk management plan. You can find the sample Risk Management Plan template in Appendix B.

Methodology Define the methodology that will be followed for managing risk for the project. This will include the process to identify risks, document the impact, and develop the risk response.

Monitor and control Define how each risk will have to be monitored throughout the project. Each risk will have a team member responsible to monitor and report on the status. Describe the process to identify a new risk, to revise risk scores, and/ or escalate a risk that reaches its triggers.

Roles and responsibilities Define the roles and responsibilities for risk management for the project, including who will identify risks, score and interpret the risks, create the risk responses, and update and publish risk response plans.

Analysis process Define the analysis process for the risks. This will include the scoring method that will define the impact and probability of each risk. For example, you could apply a simple value of High, Medium, or Low to each risk impact and probability. This section will also include the formula to determine the risk score.

Threshold Define the method that will identify which risks will be continually monitored and which will be reviewed periodically. For example, risks with the greatest impact and probability may be monitored more rigorously than the risks with the lowest impact and probability.

Budget process Define how the budget impact of risk will be identified and entered in the project budget. Does the company have a defined contingency reserve that it applies to all projects, or do you need to estimate budget impact based on the high-scoring risks?

Reporting Define the risk analysis matrix format. List the location where it will be maintained and the frequency of distribution. Define the format of risk reporting if you need to maintain risk lists on executive dashboards.

Creating a Risk Response Plan

Our nature as PMs is to be proactive rather than reactive. We prefer to develop collaborative solutions with our project team rather to develop autonomous solutions. Therefore, the preferred approach to risk management is for the project team to develop the risk response. To develop any risk response plan, you need to follow these four steps:

1. Identify risks.

2. Analyze risk.

3. Create a response plan.

4. Define the monitor and control process.

CONTRACT RISK RESPONSE

Let's say you have a project that requires an executed contract prior to installation. The identified risk is that you need to have the contract written, negotiated, and executed in 90 days. Analysis shows that the risk has a high impact to the project if the contract isn't executed on time. The company rarely executes contracts within 90 days, which results in a high probability that the risk triggers will be initiated. To mitigate the risk, you start contract negotiations early. The team member who is monitoring this risk finds out during contract negotiations that the attorney is going on a month-long cruise next week. The control process describes the risk escalation process, and another attorney is briefed on the contract so that the negotiations can continue without delay.

Identifying Risks

To identify risks, the PM must adopt a Murphy's law attitude: What can go wrong, will go wrong. This is the one time in the project where you get to be a little paranoid, dreaming up all that could possibly go wrong in the project. This is another opportunity where you should involve the project team to brainstorm the project risks. You can use a standard risk matrix as a place to start the brainstorming session with your team. If you don't have one yet, you can start one now. The following are some examples of common risks you need to review for your project:

Dates Is the date you're working to a promised date, one defined by an uncontrolled event, or the date you determined based on the tasks of the project? It's amazing how often we make ourselves crazy managing a project to a date to support a manager's promise to a client.

Culture Companies are continuing to increase their international holdings. The result is that your project team may not only be in different states but may also be on different continents. If that's the case, the project risks need to include potential cultural issues.

Business justification How was the budget for the business justification created? Was it based on historical data or "out-of-the-blue" guesses? Will the project team participate in creating the project estimates, or is the business justification budget a firm figure?

Quality standards What are the quality standards for this project? If they're very high, the risks to the project are also high. Projects that follow Six Sigma allow for only 3.4 defects per million opportunities. You need to develop strong quality strategies to ensure compliance. I'll discuss quality strategies in more detail in Chapter 8, "Defining the Procurement Management Plan."

Legal documents Do you have to execute legal documents as part of this project? Are there standard company templates, or will you have to use the other company's templates? Once you have the first draft of the document reviewed by all the parties, can you pull them into the same room to avoid the churn of review and change that accompanies the legal document process?

Procurement Do you have to buy equipment? Will the equipment be off the shelf, or will you need to develop detailed specifications for a special order? What's your company's procurement process? Do you have to go out for bid or use an approved vendor list? Is your preferred vendor even on the list? Do you have the authority to get this procurement started?

Weather and holidays Look at your project and the expected completion dates. Could snowstorms, hurricanes, earthquakes, or volcanic eruptions impact those dates? Recent history has shown all of us the value of backup communication methods and succession escalation plans. Risks associated with holidays include reduced resources because of vacations and inconvenient travel and shipping arrangements.

NOTE   For more information on Six Sigma, go to www.isixsigma.com.

Analyzing Risks

Now that you have the list of potential risks, it's time to analyze each risk for probability and impact. The risk response plan is the primary tool you'll use to track the risks and their subsequent rating. The risk response plan contains the list of potential risks for your projects and employs your chosen methodology for risk analysis; see the Risk Response Plan template in Appendix B.

The *probability* rating is based on the chance that the identified risk will occur. If you're planning an Atlantic cruise in May, a high probability exists that a hurricane may impact your trip. The *impact* rating is based on the effect the risk would have on the project. In this example, a hurricane would have a major impact the ability for the cruise ship to launch. The method you'll use to measure the probability and impact were defined in the risk management plan. These ratings will be derived by subjective team consensus.

NOTE   Don't forget to talk to your fellow PMs to compare risk response plans so that all of you can learn from each other's projects.

One question you need to answer before you begin your risk analysis is, What is the company's and the sponsor's risk tolerance level? *Risk tolerance* is the amount of risk one is willing to take to get the expected benefits. The company risk tolerance is usually influenced by the industry and determined by executive management. Some companies invest heavily in research and development, which are high-risk endeavors. Other companies only provide proven technology. If you are in a risk-adverse industry such as the nuclear or medical industry, your risk response plan will be longer, and management will be much more likely to give you the time to perform detailed risk analysis. Sponsor and stakeholder risk tolerances are personal choices. Some people are willing to rock the boat to try a new approach, and others are uncomfortable with change and risk. The reason you need to know the risk tolerances of the company, sponsor, and stakeholders is that this is what you'll use to determine the level at which you will need to develop and implement risk contingency plans. For example, a hospital has a low tolerance for risk because the risk consequences could impact life and death. Shopping centers have risk tolerances based on revenue impact.

If you review previous projects, you'll see that risks tend to occur more frequently in earlier phases and dwindle out toward the end of the project. However, the closer you get to the end of the project the greater the impact. For example, you're going on a road trip and the car's odometer is at 99,400 miles. You're due for your 100,000-mile checkup but decide to wait until you get back from the trip (which will add another 1,800 miles to the reading). Guess what happens on the road? The timing belt breaks. You are now in a strange town with a broken-down car where you have to find a mechanic familiar with your vehicle. So you're stuck in a run-down motel for three days while they do repairs. Oh, and it's a small town, so they have to order the parts. The risk could have been mitigated by getting the service done before you left, which would have delayed your trip only a couple of hours rather than the 3–4 days extension.

Defining Your Risk Response

The project team needs to identify a *risk response* for every identified risk. This is the plan that describes how you'll manage each risk. Included in that plan is the *trigger* or a warning flag that will let the risk monitor know it's time to activate a contingency plan. *Contingency plans* are what the team will do to minimize the impact of a risk that's realized. The first step in completing the risk response plan is to decide which strategy you're going to apply to each risk. The following are the recognized strategies:

Avoid risk This strategy is used when the project team decides to eliminate the risk in order to avoid any impact to the project. If you're responsible for planning the company picnic, for example, one of the project risks is that it will rain on the day of the picnic. To avoid that problem, you can have the picnic in a pavilion located in a park.

Transfer risk Transferring the risk is a strategy that doesn't eliminate the risk but moves the responsibility to another entity. This option usually falls into either contracting tasks or purchasing insurance. Both of these risk transfer options may create other risks, known as *secondary risk*. The project team decides to use a caterer for the food at the picnic rather than coordinate a potluck affair. You've transferred the risk of having enough food to a caterer, but you now have a secondary risk of the catering company going out of business the week before the picnic.

Mitigate risk Mitigating a risk is a decision to define a plan to reduce the risk to a more reasonable level. For example, scheduling the company picnic in August would reduce the chance of rain.

Accept risk The project team and the sponsor may choose to accept the risk. For these risks, the team must define triggers and contingency plans. You may decide that the risk of rain is low in August and decide to merely accept the risk of rain for the company picnic. The trigger for the contingency plan would be that it's raining the day of the picnic and a notice is sent to all employees that reschedules the picnic.

NOTE   The resulting risk analysis may warrant changes to the project plan.

Monitoring and Controlling

You've now analyzed each risk and determined your response plan. You must assign a risk owner to track the status and escalate changes as necessary. The risk response plan will describe the processes to be followed if a risk flag is triggered, if new risks are identified, and if the risk score must be revised.

This section of the plan needs to describe how often risks will be formally reviewed. For example, on a six-month project high risks should have status revisions weekly, and low risks can be reviewed only every month.

Getting Risk Management Response Plan Resistance

Will there be resistance on the risk response plan? Yes, there will, because management always *thinks* they already know all the important risks before they approve the projects. In reality, management usually knows only some of the high-impact high-probability risks. It's up to the PM to share all the critical risks and response plan with the stakeholders. This is another reason to know your sponsor, as you'll need to know if they want only a high-level executive version of risks or if they want the detailed version.

PUBLISHING THE RISK RESPONSE PLAN

Review your risk response plan. Can you think of any other risks to add to the matrix? Do the probability and impact scores match the company risk tolerance? Have you developed the appropriate level of contingencies and mitigation strategies? This is where you apply critical thinking to find weaknesses and inconsistencies in the plan. Adjust the risk response plan to accommodate any revisions that are identified during project planning.

Once the risk response plan is reasonably complete, you'll implement the risk management plan and begin the monitor and control process for risk management. This includes periodically reviewing the list of risks, reviewing and monitoring the response plans that have been implemented, and taking action to modify response plans that aren't working.

Case Study

Patricia has a copy of a risk management plan she used on another project earlier this year. She scheduled a meeting with her project sponsor, Laurie, to make sure this risk management process was still current. Laurie reviewed and approved the risk management plan.

Laurie and Patricia have worked together quite a bit in the past year. Patricia thinks of Laurie as a big-picture manager and suspects that she won't want to see the detailed risk response plan. However, she hasn't worked with Laurie on this kind on project before, so she asked her whether she preferred the detailed risk response plan or a higher-level version of the plan. Laurie confirmed Patricia's suspicions and stated that she wants to see only the top 10 risks listed in the weekly status report. They also talked about the risk tolerance level of the company. The company has a moderate risk tolerance because they're in a competitive technology industry. Laurie is known as a risk taker among her peers. Patricia doesn't think there are any major risk tolerance levels she needs to manage at this time.

Patricia has a list of risks she uses as a baseline to facilitate discussion with the project team. Since her team is relatively small, she scheduled a meeting with the entire team to brainstorm project risks. In addition to the expected risks, the team knew of a risk pertaining to the market shortage of a single-source motherboard. The motherboard is an integral part of the hardware that will be installed for Brown Enterprises.

The risk management plan defined that each risk will be scored as a High, Medium, or Low for both probability of occurrence and risk impact to the project. Once each risk was scored, the team decided that a risk response plan would be developed for any risk that had a High-High, High-Medium, Medium-High, or Medium-Medium rating. The team quickly came to consensus on the probability and impact ratings for the risks using the High-Medium-Low rating scale. Quite a bit more discussion took place pertaining to the risk strategy they would assign to each risk. Several team members said it would be a better strategy to outsource the installation of the hardware, but others said the client was too critical to risk an outside source. Both options were escalated to the project sponsor, and she decided to keep the installations in house.

The team members were assigned risks to monitor and report status. The team decided, based on the list of Medium- and Low-rated risks, that a quarterly review would meet the needs of the project.

The risk management plan and the risk response plan were filed in the online project folder and an e-mail sent to the stakeholders to notify them of the locations of the documents.

CHAPTER 4

Drafting Your Dream Team

In the previous two chapters I described the process of creating the proj ect scope statements and defining the risk management plan. Both chapters recommended you use the project team to create help these documents. So why do I now discuss drafting your dream team? I'm discussing this because this is another example of where these project-planning steps occur simultaneously. More than likely, you'll be drafting your project team as you're creating the initial scope statements. By the time you're validating project requirements, your team should be ready to go.

Have you ever worked with a team where the communication flowed effortlessly? Perhaps the team members had the utmost respect for each other and the synergy was amazing. You couldn't wait to get to work in the morning because you were energized and enthusiastic about working on the project. The result was a productive team that had a lot of fun. You get these kinds of teams through a disciplined selection process and a documented communication management plan. In this chapter, I'll show how to put together the best team based on your type of project and your organization.

Who was the original Dream Team? They were a group of highly skilled professional basketball players, with diverse backgrounds and skills, who were able to work together flawlessly in the 1992 Olympics to exceed all expectations. They became legends by raising the bar higher than anyone could have anticipated. Other than the basketball part, doesn't this fit the description of your dream team? Let's examine some processes that will enable you to create your own dream team.

Identifying Your Organization

To begin, you have to identify the type of organization you work for in order to identify how the authority for the PM, sponsor, and project team will be allotted. Many companies are hierarchically organized by function such as marketing, engineering, operations, human resources, and customer service. Let's call these *functional organizations*. In a functional organization, employees report to one manager, who reports to another manager, and on up the chain of command. The *functional managers* are responsible for all the work assigned to the employees, including all of their salary rewards as well as any discipline. Projects that take place within a functional organization often carry with them the strain of cross-department tension. For example, if a project requires the use of members from several departments, whoever manages the project will facilitate the selection of processes that will be used for this project. If all the departments follow the same processes, then you'll have no problem. But if the different departments follow dissimilar processes, any process selection will create tension.

Matrixed organizations have employees reporting to one functional manager while also reporting to one or more project managers. In matrixed organizations, projects are managed by PMs that either have to negotiate for a team or have a project team assigned to them. PMs don't usually have a lot of power in this type of organization (formally referred to as a *weak matrix*), as functional mangers give most of the formal employee rewards. In these organizations, a PM's personal influence will be a major factor that can make or break the team productivity and success. The PM needs to work within the culture of the company for appropriate informal rewards, but I've always found that supplying food at a meeting contributes to improving personal influence.

Often with smaller projects, the company has several standing teams ready to work on similar kinds of projects. A standing team is a combination of a functional organization and a matrixed organization, because the team often reports to a functional manager and the PM is brought in just to manage this project. The good news is that standing teams are accustomed to working with each other. They are likely familiar with this type of project, so training is usually not an issue. The PM may be new to the team, which can be either good or bad depending on the chemistry of the team. The team may work well together. Or the team may come complete with an apathetic attitude because the members are bored with what they're doing or they create excitement by making everything an emergency.

ADRENALINE RUSH TEAMS

I was in charge of implementing the preventive maintenance program at a power plant. I presented the team with a lot of data that showed increased efficiency in plants with a high ratio of preventive to corrective maintenance, decreased maintenance costs, and corresponding increased equipment availability. Yet the team continued to work only on corrective maintenance and ignored preventive. The problems that required corrective action were identified between 5 A.M. and 7 A.M., so as soon as everyone got to work they had to huddle and quickly develop plans to implement equipment fixes to "save the day." The team was rewarded for working on corrective measures because everything was done at a fast, exciting pace, and everyone left work feeling like they accomplished something productive every day.

Unfortunately, preventive maintenance, such as changing oil in compressors, just isn't as exciting or fun. I was able to change the culture by setting aggressive preventive maintenance goals and giving little credence to any work done on corrective tasks. To add interest, I set up smaller teams and gave them the challenge and authority to significantly improve the preventive maintenance procedures. This wasn't a quick process, but the rewards were worth the time and energy.

Apathetic teams can be turned around if you can bring something new and exciting into the project. It's more difficult if you have a team addicted to the adrenaline rushes that come with constantly putting out fires. This is a team that resists planning because *everything* they do is an emergency. It doesn't matter what tasks you assign them, the scheduled tasks aren't done because there was another emergency to handle every morning. It takes time, energy, and patience to change the attitude and behavior of these teams.

Team Composition

A perfect team should be small, natural, and diverse. The perfect number of members in your team is a personal preference. The smaller the team, the better the chance you have for better communication, as I'll discuss later in this chapter in the "Project Communication" section.

A natural team is one that effortlessly works together well and creates synergy. It's a team made up of members who like each other, respect one another, and communicate easily as a group. The term *natural team* implies that this happens occurs easily and frequently. However, neither is true. Natural teams need to be nurtured by a PM who carefully selects compatible, skilled team members who share the vision for the project. Additionally, natural teams are a rare occurrence even when a PM has the opportunity to handpick the team. As an eternal optimist I always strive to create natural teams.

Many tools are available to help you identify and select diverse team members: Myers Briggs, Emergenetics, or Personalysis. Understanding one or more of these methods can help you understand the dynamics that occur between people in team settings. This can also help you to identify skills or thought processes you need for a project.

Scheduling your project team to take personality tests is often outside the scope of a project, particularly the smaller projects. However, most of the companies I've worked for have a preference for a specific personality test and already have the results for many of their employees. You may be

TOOLS FOR TEAM BUILDING

I inherited a team of eight people who had worked together for 12 years. I was the new member to the group and was brought in to change the culture. The corporation used Myers Briggs for team development and I decided this was a good opportunity to use the tool. The team took the test and we brought in the Myers Briggs coach to facilitate the explanation of the results. There were six ISTJs, one ISFJ, one ISTP and me, an ENTJ. After the explanation of the attributes, we did an exercise where we were to place ourselves on an imaginary grid in relationship to the team on each attribute. The first attribute was Introvert-Extrovert. My team placed me on the Extrovert scale so far away from the rest of the team that I had to stand in the hallway. The same occurred for every individual that was the single representative of an attribute. The coach was able to explain to the group the positive insights that each the individual brought to the team. The best part was that she was able to suggest communication techniques that would encourage the diverse input of each team member. The team I inherited had splintered into small factions that did not communicate well or solve problems as a team. After the Myers Briggs training, the team began to communicate and develop solutions that not only resolved the current issues but also provided long-term process improvements.

For more information on personality assessment tools, refer to the following:

Myers Briggs: www.personalitypathways.com/type_inventory.html

Emergenetics: www.thebrowninggroup.com/TheBrowningGroupIntl/3.0_emergenetics.htm

Personalysis: www.personalysis.com

able to use these test results to create a diverse project. Let's walk through an example how a diverse team will give you the best project solution. Let's say you love to have big parties in your backyard, so you decide you need to re-landscape your backyard. You're the PM for this project and need to select a team. You're obviously the people person on the team. You want your landscape architect to be creative and to think creatively. Your sprinkler contractor needs to be very detailed so that everything gets watered and none of the system leaks. And finally, the general contractor needs be a person who pays attention to the schedule, procedures, and costs. Viola! You've just defined a diverse team that will give you a creative landscape that's easy to maintain and complete on schedule.

NOTE   While diversity will improve the outcome of a project, the team *must* have a shared vision and a respect for everyone on the team or the diverse perspectives may result in chaos.

I don't recommend selecting a team that's just like you. While this is always a tempting option, you won't get the multifaceted perspective you should be seeking. Diverse teams are more difficult to manage, as they continually challenge your management skills. If you're an extroverted big-picture manager, it's easier to get into a room with like-minded people and brainstorm ideas. But you also need the detailed, introverted critical thinkers to fill in all the details in the project.

Defining Skills

Before you meet with any functional managers to negotiate for your team, you need to be prepared to clearly state what skills you need to complete your project. Start with a list of tasks or groups of tasks and the hard or technical skills you know you need to complete those tasks, and complete the matrix shown in Table 4.1. If possible, identify the skill level required to complete the tasks. If you don't know the specific technical skills necessary to complete the tasks, the functional managers should be able to supply that information. Be realistic and reasonable when defining the skill levels necessary to complete the tasks because not every task requires the best of the best. After all, you don't need a rocket scientist to stuff envelopes. But you do need a nuclear physicist to design a nuclear power plant.

TABLE 4.1: Hard Skill Matrix

HARD SKILL TASK	SKILL REQUIRED	SKILL LEVEL (H-M-L)	NUMBER OF EMPLOYEES NEEDED	ASSIGNED TEAM MEMBERS
Landscape design	Xeriscape design	H	1	Tim
Sprinkler design and installation	Experience in sprinkler installations	H	3	Jaymie, Jim
Ground preparation	Spread fertilizer, level ground	M	2	Cody, Tyler
Sod installation	Lay sod	H	2	Troy, Dan

Next, create the list of soft skill attributes, such as communication skills; experience with other team members; the ability to work well with others; a compatible work ethic; a big-picture, detail-oriented, technical thought process; and people oriented. The soft skill list is a tough sell to use with functional managers to justify team selection because most companies still focus on hard skills and believe that soft skill evaluation is not necessary for team selection. However, this is a list that a PM needs to keep in mind as they assemble the team. If you thought about your most successful project teams, I suspect you'll find you had a cross-section of soft skills on your team (refer to Table 4.2).

TABLE 4.2: Soft Skills Matrix

TEAM MEMBER	THINKING PREFERENCE	COMMUNICATION STYLE	ORGANIZATION SKILLS	PROCESS SKILLS
Tim	Creative, big picture	Extroverted: storyteller	Medium to low	Medium

TABLE 4.2 CONTINUED: Soft Skills Matrix

TEAM MEMBER	THINKING PREFERENCE	COMMUNICATION STYLE	ORGANIZATION SKILLS	PROCESS SKILLS
Jaymie	Detailed, technical	Introverted: quiet	High	Medium
Troy	Big picture, Technical	Extroverted: good explanations	High	High

You need to review one more topic before you can meet with any functional managers. How will you train the team? Can you afford to offer training to those who don't have the skills you need, or should you wait until the experienced people are available to complete the tasks? Should you hire consultants who already have the skills now and train employees later?

NOTE   Keep in mind that this project may not be the only time you need people with these skills, and a decision that will get this project done early may not be the best long-term decision for the company.

Negotiating for Your Team

Now that you have the list of skills needed for your project, identify the people you really want on your team. Ask for your preferred team members when you begin to negotiate for your team, or you won't get them. I can't tell you how many times people guffawed at the audacity of my team list, yet I walked out of the team assignment meeting with everyone I requested. Schedule face-to-face meetings with the appropriate functional managers, and remember to present the compelling story about what's in it for them to give you your preferred team.

During negotiation, continually refer to your detailed list of the skills needed. This helps to minimize the chance of being assigned apathetic employees or those who are coasting until they can retire. Emphasize the desire to have team members who want to do the project.

The most common pressure you'll get for team selection is to have a team by representation. These are teams created by assigning at least one person from every potentially affected department. Often the department representation has already been determined before you're assigned to the project. When this happens, you may end up with a huge team of people who don't really care about the project but have time to attend project meetings. And that's all they'll do is attend the meetings. What often happens with this kind of team is that two or three people do all the work, and the rest of the team sits on the sideline and criticizes how the project is going. In my opinion, this is the most difficult type of project team to manage. The few people doing the work feel demoralized and resent doing all the work. The team is so huge that the PM spends an inordinate amount of time resolving communication issues usually based on misunderstandings of the project purpose. For those team members who are just attending meetings, this is a cakewalk assignment, and they have no desire to complete this project on schedule. These are the kinds of projects that go on and on and on. The corporate culture usually drives the need to have department representation on all project teams. Somehow the belief has been reinforced that the more the merrier and the better the product. The reverse is almost always the case. This corporate team culture is almost impossible to overcome, but you can select a small core team to work the project and disseminate information to the entire team through another communication process.

Team Development Stages

Once you have your team selected, it's critical to understand the stages of team creation. All teams move through forming, storming, norming, and performing stages. This is an old concept that bears reviving.

Think about a team you were recently on. In the beginning, the *forming stage*, everyone politely talks about what's happening with the project and shares bits of information about themselves. This is where names and faces are put together. Forming is usually a quick stage and can be accomplished through the first team kickoff meeting. If you've ever wondered why team start-ups use icebreaker exercises, this is the reason. The many books on icebreakers can give you creative ideas for team start-up. If you try to skip the forming stage, you'll be stuck here for quite a while until the team learns enough about each other to move to the storming stage or the team frustration grows to a level that the team begins to fall apart.

As the team start-up process continues, the group begins to get anxious to figure out where they fit into the team structure and moves into the *storming stage*. Who is at the top? What's my role? Do I know anyone on the team, and do I like to work with them? As the team members become more comfortable with each other, they will begin to jockey for position and status within the team. During this phase, the PM needs to keep the team focused on the goals and on building trust by encouraging respectful questions and open discussions. It's during this stage that conflicts may arise. The PM's role is as a mediator for these conflict-resolution sessions. These conflicts must be resolved, or the team won't move onto the next more productive stage. Depending on the makeup of the team, this stage can go on for quite some time. If the team can't move out of this stage, the PM needs to evaluate the need to change team membership. Team meetings for teams that are stuck in this stage often feel like continuous battlegrounds. Small issues turn into insurmountable problems, and you'll rarely get consensus on even commonplace issues.

Once the team has worked through the storming stage, it will move into *norming stage*. This is the first phase of performance. You'll know when the team has moved into this phase when there's friendly and appropriate teasing. The team is now comfortable with one another and their own positions, which results in the team successfully accomplishing tasks that meet the requirements and goals of the project. You'll see in this stage that the team readily obtains input from the requisite team members to jointly resolve issues and make decisions. Complex problems almost create energy as the team works to resolve the situation.

And finally, if you're lucky, you'll have a team that moves into the *performing stage*. This is the place of project nirvana where communication flows, creativity abounds, and projects are completed almost effortlessly. These teams are built on respect, harmony, and trust, which results in synergy. These are the best teams to work with, but unfortunately teams that reach the performing stage are rather rare.To clarify, this doesn't mean that most teams don't perform, but rather that most teams to not reach the supercharged level of performance of performing stage teams. As described previously, the teams that reach the performing stage are most often natural teams.

The team development stages are a tool that a PM can use to troubleshoot the lack of productivity with a team. This may be caused by a team that's stuck in a stage. At this point, the PM needs to develop strategies to move the team into the appropriate stage. Also, if any member of the team changes, the team development process starts over (see Figure 4.1). Having a team continually start over in the forming-storming cycle is one of the main reasons you need to spend a lot of energy keeping the team together. Teams that are in constant team member instability never get to norming much less performing.

FIGURE 4.1: The forming, storming, norming, and performing team stages

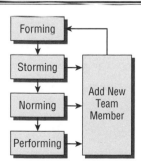

What can you do if the team membership changes? The PM needs to pull the team back together and do another kickoff. However, with these smaller projects, that isn't often possible. In that case, you have to do an individual coaching session with the new member who reviews the entire project plan, status, and issues. Then personally introduce the new member to each team member one on one.

Project Hiring

Three reasons exist why you may need to hire people for a project. The first is that you need to hire additional staff to complete this project. Second, you need to hire contractors for specific skills that are needed to complete the project. The third reason is that you need to hire employees as a deliverable for the project. Employees hired as a deliverable of the project are usually technical support or customer service positions required to support the product once it has launched. Whatever the reason, you'll need to follow your company hiring processes and incorporate the timeline into your schedule.

PMs often forget how long it really takes to hire employees, or maybe we hope it won't take as long this time. Most companies require an internal posting process prior to posting outside the company. If you are certain no qualified internal candidates exist, you may be able to convince your human resources department to post internally and externally simultaneously. This option can reduce the hiring process by several weeks. If you can get through the hiring process in less than 60 days, you should count yourself lucky.

For many projects, you often don't have time to hire and train new employees and still complete the projects on schedule. If this is the case, you'll need to be creative in obtaining internal resources to accommodate the short time constraint.

The following is a reminder of the checklist for your timeline:

- Define the need, and write a job description (estimate one week).

- Obtain approval for a new hire (estimate three days).

- Write the job posting (estimate three days).

- Post the job inside the company (estimate two weeks).

- Obtain and review the résumés (estimate one week).

- Interview internal candidates (estimate one week).

- Post outside the company (estimate two weeks).

- Obtain and review résumés (estimate one week).

- Interview external candidates (estimate one week).

- Review your choices, check references, and make offer (estimate one week).

- New hire accepts offer and gives two weeks' notice to current employer. Order equipment for office (two to four weeks).

- It's the first day; begin training.

If the new hires are a deliverable of the project, you may not be the hiring manager. But the hiring manger will need your help to make sure they stay on schedule. Hiring managers usually forget or underestimate how long it takes to hire and train new employees to support a new product. Rarely do these managers identify the employee training or new equipment ordering as part of the timeline.

Defining Team Roles and Responsibilities

Once you've built your team, each team member needs to know and understand their roles and responsibilities. For this discussion, roles are defined as who does what, and responsibilities are defined as who decides what. Define decision-making responsibility at the lowest possible level. One of the primary reasons you're writing this project plan is so the team has enough information about the project that they can make most of the decisions about the project without escalating them. Developing responsibility charts is useful to describe the major tasks, deliverables, and team member responsibilities. High-level team roles and responsibilities are fairly standard and can be reused from project to project and are reviewed in the following sections (see Table 4.3).

TABLE 4.3: Team Responsibilities Matrix

ACTIVITY	AUTHOR	APPROVER	COPY
Project charter	Sponsor	Sponsor	PM
Create project plan	PM	Sponsor	Stakeholders
Execute plan	PM	Sponsor	Project team
Control plan	PM	Sponsor	Project team
Approve scope changes	PM	Sponsor	Project team
Work packages	Project team	PM	Sponsor and stakeholders
Status reports	Project team	PM	Sponsor and stakeholders

SINGLE-THROAT ACCOUNTABILITY

Responsibility charts and schedules often list many people responsible for a given task. Then when the task isn't done, the responsible parties will look around the room and point at the other people on the list, claiming that those people said they had it under control. The PM is left with an incomplete activity and a reluctant list of responsible parties. I recommend you follow the single-throat accountability rule: holding *one* person accountable to complete the task.

Every project team needs a project team role matrix, which identifies each member's roles and their contact information. The following sections define the typical project team roles. Use these definitions to complete the project team role matrix (see Table 4.4)

TABLE 4.4: Project Team Role Matrix

TEAM MEMBER	ROLE	DEPARTMENT	PHONE	E-MAIL
Laurie	Sponsor	Operations	303-555-3333	L@ Volte.com
Patricia	Project manager	Engineering	303-555-1111	P@ Volte.com

Sponsor

The project sponsor is the person who has the ultimate authority over the project checkbook. This is the liaison between the client, management, and the PM. Sponsors are the ultimate decision maker regarding scope and changes to scope, which also means they ensure the project has clear direction with regard to business strategy. They're the ultimate decision maker for project issues and are the tiebreaking vote among the stakeholders. From the PM perspective, the sponsor is critical, because the sponsor gives the authority and responsibility of managing the project to the project manager. For example, if you have a sponsor who wants you to run *all* decisions by them, then you know you have little decision-making authority in the project and may be a glorified clerk. Or you can have a sponsor who just wants to know how the project is going and commits to support the PM's decisions.

Project Manager

The project manager is responsible for managing all aspects of the project. This is where the buck stops. If you don't believe me, see who is held accountable for a faltering project. The PM facilitates team collaborations to create and execute the project plan. The PM monitors and reports the progress of the project; identifies, resolves, and escalates project issues; and acts as a liaison.

Project Team Members

Each member of the team is responsible for getting their part of the project work completed on time and to communicate status in an accurate, complete, and timely manner (as agreed upon with the PM). It's also their responsibility to make sure the work aligns with department strategies and requirements. Each member is also responsible to represent their department's interest and perspectives. The project team will identify and resolve most issues and risks. Each team member is responsible to keep their functional supervisor apprised of the status of the project.

Project Stakeholders

Stakeholders are individuals and organizations that are actively involved in the project or may be either positively or negatively affected by the project. This is a much bigger list than you might suspect; it includes sponsors, management, customers, team project managers, end users, and vendors.

Two kinds of stakeholders exist: essential and nonessential. The essential stakeholders can prevent or enhance the success of a project because they're in positions of responsibility over critical tasks or decisions. Developing a stakeholder communications management plan can maximize the positive impact of these stakeholders. In addition, you need to identify the backup for these people and ensure they have effectively trained the backup person.

Nonessential stakeholders are people who have a passing interest in this project but may have an unexpected impact on the project. Identify these parties, and make sure they receive copies of project documentation. This is where you may be ultimately surprised when they clearly state that you can't go on because of a fatal flaw in your project that only they knew about but forgot to "share."

Once you've compiled the list of all stakeholders, then define their roles. Again, remember to keep this list as small as possible. Some of the stakeholders may need to be involved in all the meetings, some of them just need to be sent project communication, and some may only need to supply subject matter information from time to time. Even if the stakeholders are all supportive of the project, you'll need to determine how to make sure they all have the right information at the right time.

Some of these stakeholders may have a sabotage motive. I don't recommend you document this; however, you need to think through a strategy on how you'll identify the situation early in the process and how you'll manage the situation if it occurs. Preparation here will save you tenfold if only to avoid your shock response and knee-jerk reactions.

Subject Matter Experts (SMEs)

SMEs are people who have specific subject matter expertise or are performing work for the project but aren't continuous members of the team. As part of your effort to keep the team small, it's best to call on them as needed rather than keeping them as continual members of the team. Often these folks aren't people who like to attend meetings; if you keep their attendance at a minimum, they will be willing to help you on other projects.

NOTE   Once the team is selected, make sure you have a stakeholder contacts list, which identifies all the stakeholder names, roles, addresses, phone numbers, and e-mail addresses.

Project Communication

Now that you have all the participants in the project identified, you need to define the communication management plan. (Please see Appendix B for a Communication Management template.) If location, location, location is the realtor mantra, then communication, communication, communication is the PM mantra. Good communication is presenting the right thing at the right time to the right people in the right way. This sounds easy, but it isn't.

You need to first identify the number of lines of communication. The more people that pass information, the bigger the chance the message will be misunderstood or miscommunicated. Once you know the stakeholders, the following formula is useful to explain how complicated communication can become—the number of bidirectional communication pathways is a function of the square of the number of stakeholders. In plain English, the communication complexity increases dramatically as the number of stake-holders increases.

The following is the formula to describe this:

$(N \times (N - 1))/2$

Figure 4.2 shows the lines of communication.

FIGURE 4.2: Lines of communication

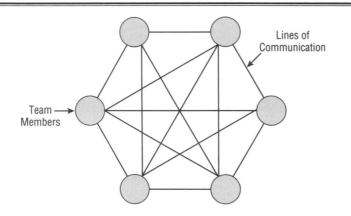

To reinforce your need to keep the team small, remember that with 5 people, you have 10 lines of communication; with 6 people, you require 15 lines; and if you jump to having a team with 10 people, you have 45 lines of communication. If at all possible, I try to keep the core team to less than 6 people. I've found a team of 6 can align their thoughts concerning the project, resolve issues, and deliver on a project on time.

You also need to remember that your team members may communicate differently because they prefer learning in different ways. Three major learning preferences exist: kinesthetic, visual, and auditory. *Kinesthetic* learners need hands-on experiences, such as personally configuring the hardware or fixing a piece of equipment. *Visual* learners can read the infor-mation and apply it to the situation. These people prefer data to be pre-sented in charts, pictures, maps, and graphics to clearly understand the message. *Auditory* people learn from verbal explanations, conversations, and storytelling. In normal populations kinesthetic learners are the most prevalent and auditory learners the least. Adults often have to use all three learning preferences to synthesize and retain the information accurately. This is why when you're working in a company with a formal, written project methodology, you may still need to verbally convey the content within the documents. Some experts claim you need to share the same information to the same person up to seven times before they're ready to hear it. This means you'll be saying the same thing over and over and over in multiple formats. It's no wonder that a PM feels like they're sharing the same information to the same people billions and billions of times.

NOTE   A major skill for PMs is to be able to have the patience to repeat the same information over and over again. Think of yourself as a "broken record," and that might alleviate some of your frustration with continually repeating yourself.

SAME WORDS, DIFFERENT MEANINGS

During meetings it's the PM's job to keep their "you're speaking different languages" antenna up. What do I mean by this? In meetings with different departments, the PM needs to be able to sit back and listen to not only what's said but also what's meant. If you can do this, you'll be able to catch some of the conversations where two people think they're communicating, but they're both talking about totally different things. For example, the customer service department is describing the requirement about receiving reports daily, and the technical teams agrees that the reports will be sent daily. Is this five or seven days a week? If you're paying close attention, you should be able to see that you need to ask the clarifying question.

One last piece to add into the communication quagmire is the team's product knowledge. Do they have different functional skills? Do they have different levels of product knowledge? Do they use conflicting department terminology? All of these will add to the complexity of communication, which leads to the need to define your communication management plan.

Creating the Communication Management Plan

Poor communication tops the list of why projects fail. If you want to be able to delegate decisions to the team, you need to define predictable communication routines. But first you need to define the types of communication you'll need to maintain for meetings, reports, issues, requirements, approvals, and escalations.

NOTE   Make sure you use clear direct communications. Innuendoes are often misunderstood and consequently confuse the intent of the message.

Then you'll need to define the frequency, formats, and location for the project communication (refer to Table 4.5). Who will contribute to each communication, and what will be the final distribution? For audit purposes, it's critical for you to track attendance at meetings and have a method for collecting and saving approvals. Some software makes it easier to capture document approvals in e-mails than others, but you still need to keep the approvals with the project documentation. Document your process in the communication management plan.

TABLE 4.5: Activity Communication Plan

ACTIVITY	AUTHOR/ FACILITATOR	APPROVER/ ATTENDEES	COPY	METHOD AND FREQUENCY
Project plan	PM	Sponsor	Stakeholders	E-mail: as changes are approved
Status reports	PM	Project team	Stakeholders	E-mail: weekly
Issue log	PM	Project team	Stakeholders	E-mail: weekly

TABLE 4.5 CONTINUED: Activity Communication Plan

ACTIVITY	AUTHOR/ FACILITATOR	APPROVER/ ATTENDEES	COPY	METHOD AND FREQUENCY
Risk analysis	Project Team	Sponsor	Stakeholders	E-mail: as risk are identified
Status meeting	PM	Project team	Stakeholders	Meeting: weekly
Document review meeting	PM	Project team	Stakeholders	As needed

Each team needs to define how they'll get decisions from the team in a timely manner. Waiting for weekly meetings to resolve issues will use up any schedule slack very quickly. Make sure you have a plan to identify when the issues are dragging on too long and how you'll resolve the problem. Short daily meetings or daily walkabouts may be your solution.

The PM needs to document problems, assumptions, and the potential resolution alternatives. After all, problem solving is mostly about accurately and thoroughly defining the problem and then facilitating a collaborative resolution.

Meeting Communication

Meeting communication requires a little extra explanation. The PM needs to identify and document the intent of weekly project meetings in the communication management plan. For example, is your weekly meeting only for status updates, or does it also include time for issue resolution? Status-only update meetings can be brief and concise. The PM can assign issue resolution outside the current meeting. Document review sessions requires that the facilitator allow questions and discussion to bounce around the room as part of the absorption process.

Most meeting facilitators underuse meeting agendas. If the meeting doesn't have a published purpose, participants may create their own undeclared agenda. Those undeclared agendas often turn the meetings into extended recreational whining sessions.

Send all agendas out a couple of days prior to the scheduled meeting. Some people are good at reading material and responding immediately. But many people need to read and process the material in order for them to actively participate in the meeting. The following are examples of meeting rules you can include in the communication management plan:

- An agenda will be prepared for each scheduled meeting, and minutes will be captured for each meeting.

- Meetings start and end on time.

- Come prepared to participate by reviewing notes prior to the meeting.

- Maintain constructive relationships.

- Avoid meeting interruptions with cell phones/pagers.

- Focus on solutions for things that can be managed.

- Look for ways to make ideas work, not reasons they won't.

- Recognize that there are many ways to do anything right. Decisions and resolutions are final. An exception is if the team overlooked an issue that would have a major negative impact on the project deliverable.

- Absence is tacit acceptance, and absence requires your follow-up.

Part of effective communicating is practicing good listening skills, which means you need to listen more than you speak. As they say, there's a reason you have two ears and one mouth. The basic listening rules are as follows:

- Show interest in the speaker.

- Let others talk.

- Keep distractions to a minimum.

- Refrain from interrupting.

- Ask questions to clarify and paraphrase as necessary.

The final section in the communication management plan should be reviewing e-mail, phone message, phone, and video conferencing etiquette. I include these in the plan because many people are still uncomfortable with new uses of technology and don't know how to effectively use these tools. It makes me crazy when people leave a phone message that says "call me," and then they race through the phone number. I can't get the answer to the question before I return the call, and I have to spend extra time trying to locate their phone number to even return the call.

Case Study

Patricia began to complete the Team Selection template (see Appendix B) to facilitate her finalization of the project team. Patricia's team includes primarily her own direct reports, so many of the team analysis sections will not be necessary.

Type of organization Volte has a hierarchical organization that prefers to use functional managers as PMs whenever it can. This gives the PMs more authority over the projects but limits the time they can spend managing each project.

The company follows an oral tradition, which will make obtaining written approvals difficult and extends the duration of all the documentation review sessions.

Team compositions Patricia has developed her skill matrix including the seven names of the Volte team members. The team consists primarily of employees with fewer than two years with the company. This means Patricia will have to spend time training the team on company process and procedures. The team already has a diverse background and diverse thinking styles.

Team skills The project team has the hard skills and the correct blend of skill levels to successfully complete this project. Patricia has used the Team Selection template to document the skill mix (see Table 4.6).

Team roles Patricia has completed the roles and responsibilities matrices for the Team Selection template. She expects there will be additional stakeholders identified as the project progresses. Patricia will add them to the matrix as necessary. The responsibility matrix is the standard matrix for her department (see Table 4.7 and Table 4.8).

TABLE 4.6: Volte Skill Matrix

TASK	SKILL REQUIRED	SKILL LEVEL (H-M-L)	NUMBER OF EMPLOYEES NEEDED	ASSIGNED TEAM MEMBERS
Create software to convert Brown Enterprises. Implement new client.	Software engineer with 16 years of experience on this platform	H	1	Jay
Create software to convert Brown Enterprises. Implement new client.	Software engineers with two years experience on this platform	L	1	Mike
Configure and install new client.	Hardware engineer with five years of experience	M	1	Christina
Configure and install new client.	Hardware engineer with seven years of experience to help develop this product	H	1	John
Configure and install new client.	Hardware engineer with one year of experience	L	1	Jodi
Write user documentation and document revised conversion and implementation process.	Tech writer and documentation control with three years of experience	M	1	Jeff
Manage project from the client side.	PM with fifteen years of experience with Brown Enterprises	H	1	Michele

TABLE 4.7: Volte Roles Matrix

TEAM MEMBER	ROLE	DEPARTMENT	PHONE	E-MAIL
Laurie	Sponsor	Operations	X76654	L@Volte.com
Patricia	Project manager	Engineering	X76755	P@Volte.com
Jay, John, Christina, Mike, Jodi	Team member	Engineering	X77755	E@Volte.com
Jeff	Team member	Documentation	X77654	J@Volte.com
Michele	Team member	Brown Enterprises	405-555-6666	MB@BE.com
Sharyl Kay	SME	Legal	X78909	S@Volte.com
Marybeth	SME	Purchasing	X79098	M@Volte.com

TABLE 4.8: Volte Responsibility Matrix

ACTIVITY	AUTHOR	APPROVER	COPY
Project charter	Sponsor	Sponsor	PM
Project plan	PM	Sponsor	Stakeholders
Execute plan	PM	Sponsor	Project team
Control plan	PM	Sponsor	Project team
Approve scope changes	PM	Sponsor	Project team
Work packages	Project team	PM	Sponsor and stakeholders
Status reports	Project team	PM	Sponsor and stakeholders
Project meeting agendas	PM	Project team	Sponsor and stakeholders
Project reviews	Project team	Sponsor	Stakeholders
Product acceptance	PM	Client sponsor	Project team

Negotiate Most of the team is a standing team, so there's no negotiation for those members. The team needs a technical writer for the user guides, and Patricia successfully negotiated the use of Jeff for those tasks. Jeff was in the documentation department during the other conversion project, so he will be helpful in collecting historical information.

No new hires are planned to complete this project or to support the launch of this project.

Team development process   The core team will be Jay, Mike, Christina, John, Jodi, and Jeff. Most of the core team has worked together for most of the last six months. However, Jeff is new to the group, so the team will have to work out where he fit in the team hierarchy. In addition, Brown Enterprises has identified that the client PM, Michele, will be their representative on the team. Michele will be responsible for collecting all the project information and dispersing it to the necessary people at Brown Enterprises.

There are no organizational changes identified at this time, so there should be no problems with getting the team to the norming stage within two to three weeks of the project kickoff.

Project communication   The team has eight people, including the PM. This means there are 28 lines of communication. All the communication for Brown Enterprises will filter through Michele. This will cut the lines of communication for the core team but increase risk for miscommunication potential at Brown Enterprises. To reduce this risk, you'll need to maintain a detailed list of Brown Enterprises stakeholders and make sure there are several scheduled documentation walk-through sessions during the project.

Communication plan   Patricia has included the Volte standard communication management plan in her project plan. Agendas will be sent out 24 hours before the meeting with the latest issue log. There will be weekly status update meetings. Issues are to be escalated as soon as they're identified. Documentation review sessions will be scheduled as the documents are completed for approval. Daily fifteen-minute project status meetings will be held the last eight weeks of the project. All stakeholders will be invited to attend through the teleconferencing line.

Patricia and her team are now ready to begin the estimating phase of the project.

CHAPTER 5

Finalizing Estimates and Budgets

To review, I've discussed how a PM orients their mind-set to begin to manage a project through PM reflections, which was discussed in Chapter 1. The PM then begins to create the project plan, which is the document that describes how the project will be managed. The first step in creating the project plan is to collect the objectives and scope for the scope management plan. The risk management plan describes the process to define and analyze the project's risks. The next step is to assemble the project team based on criteria defined in the team responsibility matrix and communication plan. Now you'll use the project team to expand on the scope management plan in order to create the Work Breakdown Structure (WBS) and then estimate resource requirements to complete the project tasks.

The purpose of this chapter and the next one is to describe methods for estimating, scheduling, and budgeting projects. The traditional approach is to create the WBS, create the network diagram, develop the budget, and then create the schedule. In smaller projects, the order of these events may change, and you may bounce back and forth as you uncover deliverables and tasks. Although software tools are helpful, they can often take more time to manipulate than they're worth. PMs need to decide when to use these tools and to what level of detail to use them.

Building a Bottom-Up Estimate

You probably expect to be able to create and evaluate all the details of the project and build the budget from the ground up. However, smaller projects often have a firm budget figure that has been given to the PM. Often, management thinks it's the PM's job to make the team's calculated numbers match management's top-down numbers. This process feels a bit unnatural to most PMs, as it isn't a logical way to manage projects. Still, the best approach is to go through the exercise of using all your documentation to create an unbiased bottom-up budget. Then assess how, or if, you can make the carved-in-stone figures from management work.

Work Breakdown Structure

When I first became PM, I thought creating a WBS was a waste of time. A WBS is a deliverable-oriented grouping of project elements that define the total scope of the project. It was a step you'd use if you were allowed to have all the time in the world and access to all the necessary resources to complete a project. Now I understand that this is the beginning of the activity definition and the checks and balances for your project scope and the foundation for your budget and schedule. The way checks and balances work is that you look at the same data from differing perspectives to ensure you've captured the best and most accurate information possible. Remember, the requirements you collected in Chapter 2 are the collection of characteristics of the deliverables. Now you'll look at the deliverables based on a hierarchy flow to double-check the scope statement.

To create the WBS, go get a new stack of sticky notes (you buy these by the case, don't you?). Your team is going to create a hierarchy of deliverables that will resemble a corporate organization chart when you're done. In fact, this is the project deliverable organization chart. At the top is the CEO of the project, the main deliverable. Let's say you're landscaping your yard. So the top box is Yard Landscaped. Now you fill in the rest of the organization by continuing to drill down to include what you need to do to complete a landscaped yard. In this example, illustrated in Figure 5.1, the second level contains Landscape Designed, Sprinkler Installed, Yard Installed, and Foliage Planted. Notice the format is a noun followed by a past-tense verb. You could also use Landscape Yard and Install Sprinkler, for example. The point of the discussion is that you need to decide on a format and stick to it throughout the development of the WBS.

FIGURE 5.1: Landscape WBS

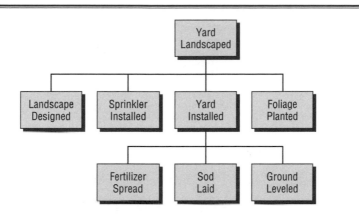

You'll continue to drill down to the next levels of deliverable detail. The details you're defining are the tasks you need to perform to complete the first-level deliverables identified in the WBS. The details may also include some of your requirements identified in the scope statement. One advantage to generating a WBS for small projects is that it's easier to delve down into a comprehensive collection of tasks. You can easily move around the sticky notes as you identify more deliverables or decide to reorganize the hierarchy. In this example, your original second level included Sprinkler Installed, but as you collect deliverables, you may find that it makes more sense to move that deliverable to the third level under Yard Installed, illustrated in Figure 5.2. The bottom layer of the WBS is the work packages you'll assign to your team to estimate and complete. A good rule is to not go more than six levels deep and to keep work packages to no more than 80 hours each.

When you're comfortable with the WBS, validate your WBS against your scope statement documents. At this point, be prepared either to update the scope statement document based on the deliverables identified in the WBS or to update the WBS based on additional deliverables triggered by the scope statement.

NOTE   Remember, if it's not listed in the WBS, it isn't in the scope of the project.

FIGURE 5.2: Revised landscape WBS

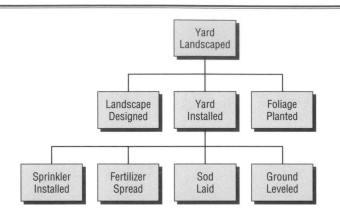

Now number each of your deliverables. You can use any method you prefer, but an outline format is usually the easiest method to apply and manage. In addition, an outline will tell you at a glance where the deliverable belongs in the hierarchy of the project. Figure 5.3 shows the numbers for your landscape project.

FIGURE 5.3: Numbered landscape WBS

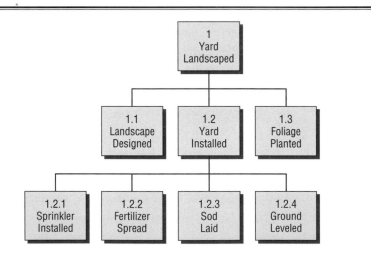

Methods of Estimating

Three basic types of estimates exist that have varying levels of accuracy: top-down estimates, bottom-up estimates, and various mathematically derived estimates.

Top-down estimates (also known as *analogous estimates*) are the estimates you'll use for the business justification. These are high-level "guesstimates" that are based on experience and on past projects that are similar in size and scope to the project being estimated; they earn the lowest confidence rating. You should use top-down estimates only to say "yea" or "nay" to the project.

WORKING WITH CARVED-IN-STONE ESTIMATES

Picture this: A PM is invited to a strategy meeting. During the evaluation of potential projects, the PM is cornered and pressured for an estimate of a potential project. The project is described by a sound bite with few details. Something like, what would it take to convert the corporate logo from green and white to red, white, and blue? The PM runs through what it took the last time she changed the company logo, adds some inflation, and gives a time frame and a cost. She also states all the appropriate language about how this is a rough estimate that will require a full analysis before she could commit to a cost and that this estimate could be off by as much as 90 percent. Unfortunately, no one in the room has heard a word since she stated the date and cost. So the PM shouldn't be surprised when this budget is handed back to her with the project assignment.

Bottom-up estimates are done by the people who are doing the work and are based on their experience, incorporating their skill at completing the work package and factoring in their availability. These estimates are done on each work package and then added together to come up with an estimate.

(See the Budget Spreadsheet template in Appendix B.) There should be a high confidence level in these figures, as this information will be used to complete the budget and the schedule.

Mathematically derived estimates, also known as *quantity-based estimates*, are estimates that take a known time for an activity and multiply it by the number of times that activity will be done. This kind of estimate works only for projects that have repeatable tasks. For example, it takes 3 minutes to blow up a balloon and tie the string onto it, and you have 300 balloons to blow up. It will take 3 minutes per balloon times 300 balloons, which will take 900 minutes, or 15 hours, to complete this task.

Finally, computerized estimating tools exist that vary in complexity and effectiveness based on industry. If you work in an industry that has these tools, make sure you identify all the assumptions and exceptions to the standard. Let's say you work in water restoration, and the estimating tool gives an estimate for boxing books that have been damaged because of a flood. The home you're estimating has a collection of rare antique books that was kept in an air-tight climate-controlled bookcase. The standard boxing estimates will not work here.

Historical Data

So far, you've defined your objectives, goals, scope, requirements, risks, and WBS for your project. The next step is to have your team estimate the time needed to complete the work package. Take a few minutes to think through how detailed you need your estimates. Do you need to track them down to 15-minute increments like attorneys and accountants? Or can you track by full days?

Use *historical data* whenever possible, as it's the best way to collect estimates. Collect project closeout data from similar projects and review what it took to complete the projects. Identify the differences in the requirements between the old project and your project, and adjust the estimates accordingly. You may have to be creative here, as projects don't always look just like yours, but they may have similar characteristics. Your project may require a contract template that's new for your company. And you'll need to estimate the duration to create the contract. But the rest of the process of negotiating and executing a contract within your company is similar for all contract negotiations. In addition, just think how much easier it will be to defend your estimate if you can show supporting data from six other similar projects.

Your project may be similar to many others but may contain a different level of complexity. The company may manufacture and box many products, but if your project requires you to be able to brand every 1000 boxes differently, you've added complexity to your project. The team needs to develop a methodology to account for the complexity difference. In this case, you'll need to send additional labels through legal, marketing, and finally print prior to sending them to manufacturing to add to the product.

Let's spend a couple of minutes talking about estimates for Research and Development (R&D). By their nature, many of the R&D tasks and corresponding estimates for the projects are unknown. R&D estimates require the ability to predict the future. Historical data will only help to say how long it took to create an innovative solution before. This solution may take longer or may not appear at all. This doesn't mean you shouldn't estimate the project. But these kinds of projects need to identify many more risks and assumptions as part of the project plan.

Figure 5.4 shows the Task Analysis template. You should have the appropriate person use a Task Analysis template to estimate the resources required to complete the work package. The task estimator should include the following:

- The list of activities necessary to complete the specified task

- Any assumptions or risks associated with the task

- Any deliverables that will define the completion of the task

- Any interdependencies with other tasks, equipment, resources, and skills to successfully complete the task

- Milestones associated with the task, task acceptance criteria, and the approval box

FIGURE 5.4: Task Analysis template

Task Analysis

Project Title: <u>2005 Backyard Landscape Project</u>   Task Evaluator: <u>Landscape Architect</u>
Task Name: <u>Landscape Designed</u>   Task Number: <u>1.1</u>

1. Task Estimates:

2 hours to collect requirements from home owner   4 hours to revise blueprints from home owner meeting
24 hours to design landscape and draft blueprints   2 hours to review plans with other contractors
2 hours to review plan with home owner   4 hours to support landscaping plan
                                                       38 Hours TOTAL

2. Task Comments or Details: *List any comments that pertain to the task or additional activity details that the evaluator wants to capture with their estimate. This can be the analysis portion of the task.*

3. Assumptions and Risks:

Home owner has a basic list of the requirements for the landscaping project.
Only one meeting will be required after the blueprint is created for the home owner to approve the plans.
All other contractors will be hired and ready to review plans in one meeting.
No major changes will be done to the landscape design during construction.
Presume no additional revisions to the plan after home owner approval.

4. Deliverables:

Home owner approved blueprint for backyard landscaping

5. Interdependencies:

No predecessor tasks are required.   All other landscaping tasks depend on this task.

6. Resources:

Landscape architect who understands native xeroscape landscaping

7. Equipment and Supplies:

Landscape software to be supplied by architect

8. Milestones:

Landscape design drafted
Landscape design approved
Landscape design reviewed with contractors

9. Acceptance Criteria:

Approved landscape design blueprint by home owner that meets requirements identified in first meeting

10. Approval:

Home owner, Jim Smith, approves estimate 5/12/05.

Who Creates the Estimate?

The best estimates come from the people who are going to do the work. They know how to do the work. This is also one place where the project life cycle and the product life cycle overlap. Letting the team create the estimate is also giving each team member time to begin analysis for completing their tasks. For this book, I'm using the term *tasks* to describe all activities or tasks that need to be completed for these projects. So while you're estimating the task Sprinkler Installed, you're also thinking about getting the sprinkler supplies, where they will be stored until the pipe is laid, and the tools necessary to put the pipe together.

It's helpful if you've worked with your team before so you know the idiosyncrasies of each team member, how they work, and how accurately they estimate. Some people always underestimate how long it will take them to do the work, and some always apply lots of padding to the estimate. If you know your team well enough, you can adjust the estimates as necessary to accommodate individual patterns.

Using SMEs to create the project task estimates is helpful because they will incorporate all the details for the estimates. However, their estimates are often based on how long it will take them to do the work, not the average Joe who doesn't have a lot of experience with the technology. Coach them to not use themselves as the model for their task estimates.

Be careful if outside contractors are doing the estimates, as you may get only what you request. Some contractors are very ethical about their estimates and will let you know of missing requirements or invalid assumptions. Unfortunately, other contractors will estimate exactly what you ask for and then ding you with additional charges as they identify them throughout the project.

Performing an Estimate Analysis

Now that you've collected all the projected estimates for the work packages and tasks, you'll look at how they fit into the total project estimate. Picture this: You're starting a project, and you were given the same estimate given to the client. The expectation is that you can miraculously get the project done with all the known and yet-to-be-uncovered requirements within that estimate. Then you collect the requirements and find that the scope is much larger than was originally communicated to the client. Consequently, the cost of the project is also much larger. The sponsor asks you to sharpen your pencil to reduce the budget. You sharpen the pencil, tweak the budget, run it by the team, and send it back to the sponsor. But you're still too high. The sponsor asks, "Can't you get it done for half that?" You respond, "Yes, if I can cut these items from the scope." But the sponsor doesn't want you to cut the items and asks, "If you get cheaper team members, don't have any meetings, don't do any testing, and don't document anything, could you meet the estimate?" You respond, "Yes, but the project won't meet stakeholders expectations; is that okay?"

Does this exchange sound familiar? If you've been doing project management for any length of time, you've lived through this verbal exchange. This may be the beginning of sending you and your team down the "analysis paralysis" path. On this path, you and your team will spend more time analyzing, inquiring, and defending than it would take to actually complete the project. And the original number that was once only 20 percent off the target is now easily 75 percent off the target. This can happen quickly in smaller projects because you're working with such tight budget and time frames. Try to resolve these iterations between you and the sponsor while letting the team get the real work done.

Precision vs. Accuracy

You may be asking, "What's the difference between *precision* and *accuracy*?" Precision is the number that's clearly defined in minute detail. For example, say the project estimate is 450.0167 hours. The accuracy of an estimate relates to the correctness of the number. Although 450.0167 is a precise estimate, I doubt anyone is going to track their time down to the minute. However, if the project is completed in 450 hours, then the estimate was accurate, and the accuracy of your budget will be directly related to the time spent putting it together. If it's critical that the budget be within 1 percent accuracy, you'll be spending loads of time creating it, verifying it, and justifying it. But I'm talking about smaller projects here. Does it make sense to get an estimate within 2 percent for a 100-hour project? I suspect you'll spend more than the two hours trying to get the estimate accurate. As the PM, you need to be the one who can step outside the insanity and do the reality checks.

Decide the units you'll estimate to, such as half days, days, or weeks. Estimating software packages will let you estimate down to the 100th place, but does anyone really think you're going to put that into the schedule? And does anyone really think the team members will track their time down to .35 hours? Getting things that precise doesn't make them more accurate, and it may put your estimate under scrutiny by those who will question your method of obtaining such detail.

Estimating Pitfalls

Several items can eat up your budget quickly once the project starts, and they're not usually found in the task estimates. Let the team members know they need to include the following items; otherwise the PM will need to add them to the estimates after they're turned in and prior to creating the budget:

PM time   The PM time starts at the beginning of the project and continues through project closeout. Most of the time and effort is spent during planning to create the project plan, create the team vision, and set the stage for efficient project completion. Execution and control should take the least time and effort. The last couple of weeks often require more babysitting time to pull together the loose ends that appear at the end of the project. Closeout should consist mostly of PM time that includes closing documents and creating the lessons learned documentation.

Planning and estimation time   The first part of the project is spent on planning. Time spent here will reduce rework and other inefficiencies while completing the project. However, team members rarely add planning time to their estimates.

Interruption time   Remember, your team members are doing many tasks simultaneously. Every time someone gets interrupted, it will take an average person 15 to 30 minutes to get back on track. Additionally, in today's corporate world, everyone is working out of a cubicle, which encourages interruptions. If your team is located where there are a lot of interruptions, you may want to decrease your definition of workday from six hours per day to five hours per day to account for the potential interruptions. That will allow for two to four interruptions per workday (figuring on four 15-minute interruptions or two 30-minute interruptions).

Learning curve time   The PM needs to decide how much time to add to the estimate to accommodate for the learning curve for the team. The learning curve may be reduced if you can schedule time with the SMEs to work and teach simultaneously. If this technology isn't only new to your team but also to the industry, make sure you incorporate additional Quality Assurance (QA) test-fix cycles into the testing portion of the project.

Meeting time   Always remember to define time for project meetings, including meeting preparation and note publishing time. When you calculate time for meetings, you may be shocked at the impact. This is the point in the project plan where you need to decide how many people the project can afford to have attend the project meetings and who needs to read project notes to obtain status.

User acceptance testing   User Acceptance Testing (UAT) is the place where the client actually gets to see how the product works. Is this a one-hour demo, or is it time on the system to let the client pound on the features? How will your team support this UAT? I've seen testing estimates blown out of the water by not adding the team time it takes to hold the hand of a difficult client. The next question you should ask is, will the client commit to a specific test time, or will they really test it once it gets into production?

Rework time   Make sure to allow time to for the test-fix cycle, also known as *rework*. The test-fix cycle includes time for the tester to find a problem, for someone to fix the problem, and for the tester retest the fix. Your company probably has some history to determine how many times your team should cycle through the test-fix cycle for any given product release.

Setup, installation, and configuration time Different industries use these terms to mean different things, but regardless of the definition, these are tasks that need to be assigned to a team member to estimate. Sometimes these are some of the more obvious tasks that get missed until the product is getting close to installation. These tasks may also need to include test-fix cycles.

Project reviews and closeout The PM should schedule an independent review of any project that takes more than six months to complete. The review can be a simple review of project documents or include interviews with the team and key stakeholders. The intent of the review is to make sure the project is still on track based on the project plan. If you don't identify and schedule a review during planning, everyone will be so buried in the project that the project will be done before you know it. If you're off track, you missed the opportunity to adjust for it during the project.

The PM needs to estimate both the independent reviews and closeout processes based on their experiences with other projects. Make sure you include tasks for any independent project reviews and the project closeout.

Review and approval time Companies have different cultures around review and approval responsibilities. Many of the approval processes are based on the level of technology used within a company. Some companies have systems that automatically send an e-mail alert when an approval is pending, and others still use manila envelopes that have to be carried from person to person for signature. In large companies, you may need many approvals, and each approval may have a 24-hour turnaround limit. If you need to have all of these approvals before you can make any change to the scope of the project, you can see how the end date can quickly be in jeopardy. One technique you can use to mitigate this issue is to pull everyone into a room and have them approve it simultaneously.

Estimates need to be a collaborative effort between the PM, sponsor, team members, and stakeholders, as more input will yield better and more accurate estimates with appropriate assumptions. If this isn't a collaborative effort, you can end up with a war between stakeholders over what was supposed to be in the project and what wasn't. Once all the task estimates have been collected and collated, you can begin to put together the budget.

Creating the Project Budget

Now that you've collected all the work package resource requirements, it's time to collate the information into the project budget. Project budgets are the cornerstone for selecting, managing, and completing a project. Budget, also known as *cost*, is one of the triple constants used to track project success. Your project budget is based on all your completed project documentation and work package estimates. Like the rest of the project plan, this is another area that starts with high-level time and cost estimates and ends with a detailed budget that's considerably more accurate and can be used to manage all the tasks. By the time you begin to write the project plan, the high-level estimates should have already been created and used to approve the project. It's now time to drill down to the next levels of detail to create the project budget.

Just Add It Up

Just add it up. This sounds simple, doesn't it? Just take all the project planning information, add the detailed task analysis estimates, and create your project budget. It's never that simple, though, is it? First you need to be aware of your corporate processes for budgets, procurement, and Requests For Proposals (RFPs). Additionally, your budget needs to follow the correct format and align with the approval schedules. Usually you'll be assigned to work with someone in finance or accounting. They will not only help you get the project into the appropriate format for the accounting system but also help you set up processes to receive monthly expenditure reports.

Many software packages can be used for creating and tracking project budgets, but for these smaller projects a basic spreadsheet may prove easiest to maintain.

If your company doesn't have real-time expense tracking, you'll need to develop a spreadsheet to track expenses. It's the PM's job to track expenses even if you can't count on company systems for timely data.

Capital Expenditures

Large companies have stringent processes to approve and track *capital expenditures*. Capital expenditures are investments in the business that can be charged to a capital asset account defined by standard accounting practices. These expenditures add to the value of the business as assets rather than expenses. Different industries have different rules on what's in and what's out of the capital expenditure realm. With the current political environment of companies abusing their use of and tracking of funds, companies are even more careful about these processes. Make sure you know your company's philosophy, procedure, and timeline for capital expenditures. These often have a much longer review cycle or only annual approval. Start immediately on procuring capital materials as soon as you know you have a project with capital expenditures.

Non–Project-Specific Costs

The tricky part about project estimates is that you need to take into account all the *overhead* and administrative costs associated with the estimate. This includes management and facility costs. Some companies choose to annually allocate all the overhead costs into one project cost center for smaller projects, which makes it easier to estimate for each project. Other companies want you to add that level of detail into each project estimate. Overhead and administration costs can usually be applied as a percentage of the total project estimate, and that number is defined by the finance department. Obviously, the lower the allocation, the better.

Contingency reserves are additional costs added to the projects for unexpected events. This is another percentage that can be calculated based on industry or company experience. But be aware that if your project budget gets cut, the contingency reserve is the easiest target. You need to be ready to defend your rationale for adding it to the project budget. If it does get cut, make sure you add that to your risk matrix.

NOTE   R&D projects may need more contingency reserves because there are more unknowns for these kinds of projects.

Maintenance and operating costs shouldn't be part of the project budget. These figures should have been included in the high-level estimate used to justify the project. These costs will be incurred after the project has been completed. But you need to be aware of estimated costs so you can ensure the deliverables of the project can meet those expectations. In the landscaping example, there aren't expected maintenance costs for the system in five years, but you know you need to have self-draining systems and parts that won't freeze or erode.

The final step, before you submit the budget for approval, is to take one last pass where you question the numbers yourself. Use industry and company benchmarks to check your figures. Each industry has its own benchmarks for labor/material allocation. Software development is primarily labor, and construction uses 50 percent labor and 50 percent materials. Make sure you've included benefits, facility costs (lease or building fixed costs), marketing costs (including collateral or focus groups), legal costs (contracts, patents, and trademarks), travel and food, advertising, R&D, consultants, telephone charges, office supplies, Internet charges, software, hardware, and training.

The PM will complete the budget using the WBS and the Task Analysis forms. Use the task IDs and descriptions from the Task Analysis template, and complete the estimate columns accordingly. The rest of the budget spreadsheet can describe any other costs that will be attributed to the project. Figure 5.5 shows the Budget template for the landscape example.

FIGURE 5.5: Landscape Budget template

1. Task ID	2. Description	3. Estimate				4. Comments
		Labor			Materials (dollars)	
		Hrs	Rate	($)		
1.1	Design	40	$30	$1200	$0	
1.2.1	Sprinkler	80	$35	$2800	$3000	
1.2.2	Fertilizer	16	$12	$192	$300	
1.2.3	Sod	48	$25	$1200	$2500	
1.2.4	Ground	16	$12	$192	$250	Material is rented equipment.
1.3	Foliage	48	$35	$1680	$3000	
	Subtotal			**$7264**	**$9050**	
	Total			**$16,314**		

Budget Template
Project Title: 2004 Backyard Landscape Project   Project Manager: Home owner, Jim Smith

5. Labor rates:

Labor rates are identified in the budget table. There will be no benefits allocated to the project, as the work is being done with contract labor.

6. Overhead:

No overhead for this project

7. Miscellaneous:

Landscape celebration party $750

8. Contingency Reserve:

Need to keep approximately 10% for additional costs of shrubs or other landscape items (such as rocks or statues). (This is $1631.)

9. Capital:

The home owner will not capitalize landscaping.

10. Total Project Budget:

$18,722.00

11. Approval:

Approved by Jim Smith, 5/20/05

Approval

This is another natural place to get sponsor approval. If you have time, review with your project team the final version of the budget prior to submission.

Schedule a face-to-face meeting with your sponsor to review the budget. Don't throw the budget over the wall and hope that someone recieves the report and understands what you submitted. You *need* to have the sponsor's support here; otherwise you'll be on your own to defend the use of approved dollars. The project budget approval will be used as the *cost baseline*, and any approved changes to the expenses will be measured against this figure.

NOTE   Spend the time to get the budget right the first time because getting more money is usually impossible.

Be prepared to defend the budget again and again and again. Throughout the project you may need to continually review and revise the budget. The lower the priority of your project, the more frequently you may be asked to adjust your budget. If you spent the time collating the information in the project plan, you'll spend less time researching alternatives later in the project.

If you're required to remove dollars and tasks from the project plan, make sure you diligently add the removed items to the risks of the project *and* track scope changes. Many times you'll end up with a project that meets the schedule and budget but doesn't meet the stakeholder expectations because those items were removed to meet the budget. While "I told you so" may not be what you say to management at the end of the project, you can use this as additional historical data for future projects. Make sure the measured consequences of these decisions are documented in the lessons learned.

Once you have formal project budget approval, review the document team and stakeholders. Stakeholder buy-in for what you're going to do and how much it will cost is necessary to meet any of the goals you've defined for the project.

Case Study

Although Patricia was given the an analogous project budget figure by Laurie, Patricia knows the value of the bottom-up estimate process. So she pulled together the project team to create the WBS. The meeting took about two hours, and the team walked away with their task analysis forms to esti-mate each assigned task. The team decided it made sense to schedule in full days and to use six hours as the definition of a full day. The justification is that the company allows for 30 minutes for lunch and two 15-minute breaks, and then there's an average of 1 hour of non-project meetings, train-ing, and administration time for performing tasks such as checking e-mail. The company has no estimating tools, so the totals will be captured and managed from a spreadsheet.

Patricia copied all the previous conversion documentation and gave it to the team to use as reference. Unfortunately, there was no requirements documentation or a WBS that the team could use as a baseline. Patricia explained to the team the value of using the task analysis exercise as the beginning of analysis for the project.

The project team completed the task analysis for all the tasks. The estimate for completing the tasks was 1235 hours. Labor costs were an average $70 per hour. A company standard of 42 percent for labor benefits will need to be applied to the salary figure, which will raise the labor costs to $100 per hour. Patricia took on the tasks of estimating the project management time for the project. She plans on spending 12 hours per week for the first 3 weeks of the project, 4 hours per week for the next 26 weeks, and then 12 hours per week for the last 3 weeks of the project. This is 176 hours of PM time to man-age this project. Based on her experience, she will spend quite a bit of time on the back end of the project making sure to tie up all the loose ends.

Because the team is working only part-time on this project, she is going to add 2 percent to all the team estimates to account for the interruptions. The team is fairly familiar with the conversion implementation process, so there will be minimal time for the learning curve.

The project team will meet weekly for an hour. The project team has 7 Volte Corporation team members who will meet weekly for 1 hour per meet-ing for a 32-week project; this adds up to 224 hours. The kickoff meeting, requirements, and WBS meeting will add 40 hours. Patricia plans to include 1 SME and 1 stakeholder in each meeting, which adds another 64 hours to the project meetings. Patricia expects it will take her 1 hour each week to prepare for the team meeting and publish the status report, which adds an additional 32 hours to the project. In total, the meetings add 360 hours to the project.

It's critical that Brown Enterprises approves all aspects of this project, so Patricia is going to schedule UAT with the client for two weeks. That will take approximately 20 hours of team support for this effort.

The QA team has reviewed the project scope and the individual team tasks and has estimated it will take the team 600 hours to test the product prior to moving it into production. This estimate includes three test-fix cycles for the conversion and configuration testing.

Patricia doesn't expect additional approvals once the project plan has been approved. However, she is planning to have an independent project review midway through the project. That will take 20 hours of another PM's time and 10 hours of team time for individual interviews. The project close-out will take 2 weeks at the end of the project, not included in the 32 weeks.

There will be no capital expenditures for this project, and there is no R & D, which can be amortized. Volte Corporation has decided to use 12 percent on all non-R&D projects for contingency reserve. In addition, the company uses 23 percent as the overhead to cover management, facility costs, and miscellaneous administration costs. This will be added to the figure once all the estimates are collected and subtotaled. The hardware necessary for the project has been estimated at $105,000.

After adding all the task analysis forms and applying the necessary non-task-related estimates, the budget for the project comes to $436,677. This estimate is 3 percent under the original estimate. Figure 5.6 shows the overview of the budget for this project.

Patricia meets with Laurie to discuss the estimate. Laurie wants to know if the estimate can be cut by an additional 10 percent. Patricia states she will manage the project as tightly as she can and says, "Laurie, if I cut the budget another 10 percent, there will be no cushion for anything that comes up unexpectedly. And you know that something always comes up. Remember the implementation last year where the client disclosed at the last minute that their system was undergoing a major rewrite, and we had to change our password format to accommodate their new system?" Laurie sighs as she remembers all the issues that were raised with the last-minute changes.

Laurie approves and formally signs the budget. Patricia sets up a meeting to walk through the final budget with her project team and to set the stage to create the project schedule.

FIGURE 5.6: Volte budget

Budget Spreadsheet

Project Title: Brown Enterprises Conversion and Implementation   Project Manager: Patricia

Description	Estimate			Materials (dollars)	Comments
	Labor				
	Hrs	Rate	($)		
All Tasks	1235	100	$123,500	105,000	
Meetings	360	100	$3600		Kickoff (64), Wkly (264), Prep (32)
Testing	600	100	$60,000		
UAT	20	100	$2000		
Project Review	30	100	$3000		
Subtotal	2421	100	$242,100		
Interruption Time	48	100	$4800		2% of tasks
Overhead	446	100	$44,600		23%
Contingency	290	100	$29,000		12%
Subtotal	3316		$331,600	$105,000	
		TOTAL	$436,677		

CHAPTER 6

Creating the Project Schedule

Project schedules have evolved from hand-drawn charts to sophisticated integrated software applications. Yet the project schedule is still one of the best tools available to manage a project to successful completion. Whether you use a detailed Gantt chart schedule, a milestone schedule, or a simple spreadsheet, employing basic scheduling techniques is the next critical step in creating an effective project plan.

The previous chapter described techniques for identifying project tasks and the corresponding resource requirements and using that information to generate the project budget. This chapter will review activity sequencing and activity duration estimating, which both culminate in schedule development. In addition, I'll review scheduling techniques you'll use while managing projects, such as compressing schedules and managing critical paths.

Introducing Activity Sequencing

Activity sequencing is the process where the project team puts tasks in the order they will be accomplished and the results in a network diagram. You'll use all the tasks you identified in the previous chapters through scope, requirements, and Work Breakdown Structure (WBS) creation to create your network diagram. This is another check and balance to verify you know all the project tasks, only this time you'll look at all the tasks in the order they'll be accomplished. During the network diagram creation process, you may again identify tasks that weren't identified during the requirements gathering and the WBS activities.

Defining the Network Diagram

A network diagram, or *precedence diagram*, is a tool used to display the sequence of the tasks that will be required to complete your project. To create a network diagram, start with a new stack of sticky notes or use the sticky notes created during your WBS process. Place the notes in the order that the tasks need to be completed. Sequencing project tasks is a skill that will take practice because most projects don't have a simple, single-threaded task sequence. The good news is that once you've mastered this skill, you'll find it's a simple, commonsense process. This is your first opportunity to identify tasks that can be worked in parallel, which can reduce the duration of the project. Also remember that task sequencing is another iterative process that will require the PM to revise the network diagram as issues are resolved, risks are identified, and new tasks are uncovered. Figure 6.1 shows the network diagram for the landscaping example from the previous chapters.

FIGURE 6.1: Landscape sequence

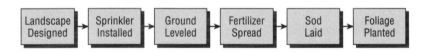

NOTE PMs and scheduling software use the terms *task* and *activity* interchangeably in their documentation and processes.

Estimating Activity Durations

This is the part of the process where the PM estimates the duration of the activities and enters the tasks into the schedule software. The duration of the tasks will be calculated automatically in the scheduling software, based on the number of hours that you choose to enter into the project calendar and the resources assigned to each task. We will now review the decisions that a PM must make prior to entering the tasks into the schedule.

Deciding on the Details

First, you'll need to decide what level of task detail you'll need in order to manage your project. Do you need detailed tasks lists or will a summary be sufficient? You can make yourself crazy by adding every little task that exists in a project. In fact, I've seen schedules that include a task for the weekly team meeting that included the following detailed tasks: "identify the date and time for a meeting," "schedule a meeting room," "create an agenda," "send meeting invitations," and "send reminder notices." Although these are all necessary activities to run an effective meeting, it will take longer to enter them into the schedule and update the status than it actually takes to complete these tasks. A task labeled "weekly status meeting" is a more appropriate level of detail for the schedule. This decision may also be based on factors such as the team or product maturity.

Second, you'll need to identify the level of detail to report to the project stakeholders. They may just want a one-page executive summary, or they may need to see all the scheduling details. The WBS outline detail is an excellent guide for defining a consistent level of detail for summary reports. For example, you can use the second level from the landscape example as a summary-level report for the stakeholders (see Figure 6.2).

FIGURE 6.2: Landscape summary report

ID	Task Name	Start	Finish	Duration
1	Yard Landscaped	1/3/2005	1/18/2005	12d
2	Landscape Designed	1/3/2005	1/5/2005	3d
3	Yard Installed	1/6/2005	1/13/2005	6d
4	Foliage Planted	1/14/2005	1/18/2005	3d

NOTE   Keep the schedule to one to two pages if you choose to send out copies. This facilitates stakeholder use of the document.

Entering Tasks into Scheduling Software

Today PMs use software, such as Microsoft Project, to create schedules, rather than calculating and creating them manually. This is where you get to put to use all the information you've collected about your tasks and create the project schedule. Take your summary-level descriptions, and enter them into the system. You'll use the task analysis forms you created while defining activities in Chapter 5 to enter the task description, the WBS number, the hour estimates, and the resources for each task. You'll use the network diagram to enter the sequence that the tasks will be performed.

Defining Activity Precedence

Before the schedule software can create a schedule that accurately reflects the order in which the tasks will take place, you'll have to create *task links*, which are easy icons to identify in scheduling programs because they're shown as links of a chain. Task links describe the working relationship that each task has with the other project tasks. *Finish to start*, *finish to finish*, and *start to start* are the primary types of task links used.

Finish to Start

The most commonly used link is *finish to start*, which means that one task must be finished prior to starting the next task. For example, if you're the PM in charge of a company picnic, you need to know the date and venue of the picnic before you can schedule the caterer. The Select Picnic Date task needs to be complete before the Select Caterer for Picnic task starts. This is the default relationship if you select a link icon (see Figure 6.3).

FIGURE 6.3: *Finish to start* task link

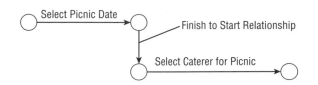

Finish to Finish

Finish to finish task links should be applied when the tasks must be completed at the same time. In the picnic example, the food and entertainment may have a *finish to finish* relationship. One doesn't have to be done before the other; they both just need to be done by the time the employees begin to arrive at the venue. The Set Up Food for Picnic task and the Set Up Entertainment for Picnic task must finish at the same time. Note that these tasks don't have to start at the same time (see Figure 6.4).

Start to Start

Start to start task links should be applied when the tasks must start at the same time. You can start to select the caterer and entertainment at the same time because you'll have all the necessary information once the date and venue has been selected. The Select Caterer task and the Select Entertainment tasks start at the same time. Note that these tasks don't have to finish at the same time (see Figure 6.5).

FIGURE 6.4: *Finish to finish* task link

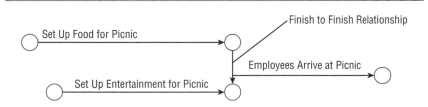

FIGURE 6.5: *Start to start* task link

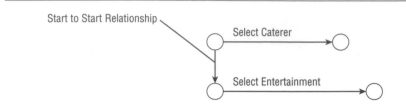

NOTE   Make sure you save the baseline schedule at this point. You don't want to start playing with schedule options and lose the original schedule.

Developing the Schedule

Now that you have the tasks and initial relationships entered into the application, it's time for you to begin working your magic. This is where you evaluate options in sequencing resources to maximize all the company resources while meeting stakeholder expectations. In other words, this is where you make sure the project is done right.

Critical Path

New PMs often ask how to stay on top of every task during the course of the project. The answer is that most PMs don't; they focus on managing only the critical path items. The critical path is the longest full path on the project. This is the absolute shortest time that a project can be completed. If you spend your time managing the activities on critical path—and keeping the critical path tasks on schedule—your project will meet the scheduled finished dates.

Let's go through a quick refresher on critical paths. The project you're planning is a room extension to an office building. The first task is the room design. Then you can break the tasks into two flows, one for constructing the room and one for decorating the interior of the room. The construction of the room can be in progress while you define and order materials for the interior decorating. The longest full path is the construction path, which is 42 days long (see Figure 6.6). The decorating path is merely 15 days long. The construction path can't be shortened because none of the construction tasks can take place in parallel with each other. For example, the foundation must be done before the walls can be done, and the exterior walls must be done before work can be completed on the interior walls. Therefore, the shortest duration of the project is 42 days. If any of the tasks on the critical path slip, the entire end date of the project will slip. If the foundation tasks actually take 18 days rather than 14 days, the shortest the project can be finished is now 46 days.

FIGURE 6.6: Critical path example

1/2	14d	1/15
Complete Foundation		
1/2	0	1/15

1/16	14	1/29
Complete Walls and Roof		
1/16	0	1/29

1/30	10	2/8
Complete Interior Work		
1/30	0	2/8

1/1	1	1/1
Design Room Extension		
1/1	0	1/1

2/9	3	2/11
Complete Interior Decorating		
2/9	0	2/11

1/2	3d	1/4
Select Color and Theme		
1/29	27	1/31

1/5	3d	1/7
Order Window Coverings		
2/1	27	2/3

1/8	5d	1/12
Purchase Furniture		
2/4	27	2/8

Legend

Early Start	Duration	Early Finish
Task Name		
Late Start	Stack	Late Finish

FOCUS ON THE CRITICAL PATH

Make sure you're focusing on managing tasks that make a differ-ence. I've known project teams that spend hours evaluating and reducing time on tasks throughout a project only to be surprised that the project finish date is the same as it always was. What hap-pened? They spent time reducing duration of tasks not on the crit-ical path. And the longest path is still the longest path. The PM needs to facilitate team sessions and focus their energy on reduc-ing critical path task durations to impact the project finish date.

In my opinion, the best feature of scheduling software is that it easily cal-culates the project critical paths. The software uses the task status to con-tinually recalculate the critical paths so you can easily see the impact to the project's end date as task dates slip or task durations increase. I keep on top of all task statuses to make sure the current critical path is being managed.

Unfortunately, smaller projects often have such compressed timelines that there are often many critical paths. This situation raises many risks. The probability of at least one of the critical tasks missing the finish date is high. This will impact the ability of the team to meet the original project's finish date. If you find your project has many critical paths, revise your risk response plan and include strategies to keep all these tasks on schedule.

Analyzing Float

Another task attribute you can use to evaluate tasks is float. *Float, or slack,* is the amount of time a task can be delayed without impacting the comple-tion date. Only tasks that aren't on the critical path can have float. If a task isn't completed on time and uses up its entire float, the task will immedi-ately become part of the critical path. Be aware of tasks that are using up their float because those are the tasks that are at risk of missing their latest finish dates. If you have a task that looks like it may move to the critical path, use your team to resolve the issue before it impacts the schedule.

Let's use the room extension example to identify tasks with float. If you refer to Figure 6.6, you can see that many of the decorating tasks have float or slack. These are the tasks that have the number in the center bottom number greater than zero. This makes sense. Even if you got the window covering and furniture early, you can't install them until the floor, walls, roof, and interior walls are done. In fact, it doesn't help the project to get all the furniture too early, because you'd have to find a place to store it until it could be placed in the finished room.

Schedule Compression

Schedule compression sounds like slow constant pressure resulting in shorter project duration. Synonyms of *compress* include *squash*, *cram*, *jam*, *stuff*, and *compact*. These synonyms are better descriptions of what the PM is expected to do with a schedule that was carefully and thoughtfully created. Requests don't come in as, "Can you reduce this schedule by a day or two?" They're dictated as, "Cut the due date by 60 days!" As the PM, you may be under extreme pressure to comply with the date reduction edict. Remember that you and your team developed the schedule based on facts. This is the time to use your negotiation and sales skills to sell management on the justification for the project dates. If you can't convince management of your position, make sure you have as much information as you can gather, as you'll have to go back and sell the new dates to your project team. If you can't present a believable justification for the new date and the team thinks the expectation is unachievable, you'll end up managing the severely damaged morale of your team and probably fail to meet the requested compressed project completion date. Make sure you communicate clearly and often with your project sponsor if this situation arises. You may want to review your project to see if you can reasonably split the project into phases and reduce the scope of the first phase to meet the expectations.

Crashing and fast tracking are the two most common ways PMs use to compress a schedule. Crashing is the process where you add more resources to complete the critical path tasks. The presumption is that if you have more people on your team, you can get the project done sooner. On paper you can always make that happen. But in real life, it takes nine months to make a baby. You can't divvy it up into one-month chunks with nine women and get it done faster. When you start getting pressure to add more people to the project team, step back and verify it makes sense to add more resources. Don't forget that by adding more people, you'll be adding lines of communication to your project. You'll also be changing the makeup of the team, which will put you back into the beginning of the forming, storming, norming, and performing cycle for team start-ups. Evaluate whether this is an effective schedule compression solution.

Fast tracking is the process where you schedule to work more tasks in parallel. This is another solution that may be limited by resources. The PM must be cognizant of the risks associated with performing more tasks in parallel. The more tasks that happen in parallel, the more chances you'll have that one group steps on the deliverables of another. In the landscape example, you can have some people planting trees the same time others are laying sod, which will get the yard completed sooner. However, rolling wheelbarrows of dirt across leveled ground can dislodge the placement of the sod rolls, which will require the sod layers to re-lay the sod. Think this through before applying this strategy excessively.

Schedules are often difficult for management to read. One reason is that usually many tasks are happening in parallel which makes it hard to decipher the important information. Management and quality assurance people have a basic belief that good project management processes have schedules that follow a waterfall approach, as shown in Figure 6.7. Waterfall schedules work where there are clear gateways that define where one phase ends and another begins. An example of a waterfall schedule would be a project where project initiation is completed and approved prior to starting any work on project planning.

FIGURE 6.7: Waterfall schedule

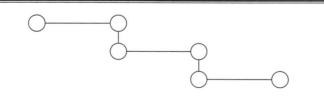

FIGURE 6.8: Resouce histograms

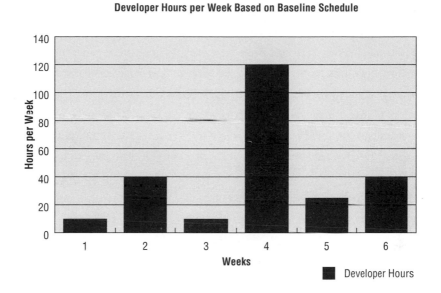

Real-world projects rarely follow waterfall schedules. Why? Project dead-lines may be compressed and inflexible, which requires the project teams to complete tasks out of order or in parallel to meet the deadlines. The shorter the project, the more compressed the tasks may appear on the schedule. And this yields even less flexibility. Many of your quality processes define clear approvals and gateways, which would imply that many projects have waterfall schedules. I've started projects where the schedule handed to me from proj ect initiation is a waterfall schedule. By the time I enter real estimates into the system, even the summary-level tasks don't form a waterfall.

A PM can use several tools to evaluate resources to compress a schedule. Resource histograms are the bar charts created from the project scheduling programs that enable you to view the use of resources over the duration of the project. Often, projects are assigned specific resources for the duration of the project. Histograms are tools to help you levelize resources. Leveliz-ing resources is the process where you spread the workload as evenly as pos-sible throughout the project. Figure 6.8 shows the initial schedule of developers based on the task analysis input into the scheduling program.

Notice that the resource requirement fluctuates from one person per day in a week to three full-time people for an entire week. If you followed this resource plan, you'd need to make sure three developers are up to speed on your project so you could use all three for one week.

The levelized view of this project resource is one where you schedule one developer for forty hours per week (see Figure 6.9). This is the optimum use of a resource. However, it doesn't take into account vacation, sick time, or backup workers if the developer critical path tasks fall behind.

Finally, resource histograms are good tools if you have many people assigned to work only on your project. They aren't as valuable for small projects with just a few people who are assigned to many projects. Why? Because histograms show use of resources for a specific time, and unless you have all of the resources for all of the projects in a single schedule program you will not be able to view the interaction and impact of resource schedules in a histogram. This may a place where a simple spreadsheet would work best to track resource usage.

FIGURE 6.9: Levelized resource histogram

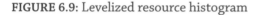

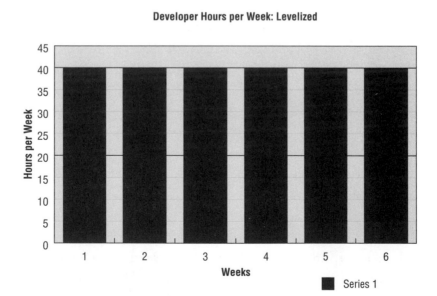

Seeing How We Really Do It

The PM best practice is to define activities, define sequence activities, estimate activity duration, and, finally, create the project schedule. Ideally, you'd be able to facilitate three meetings to collect requirements, define the WBS for activity definition, and create the network diagram for activity sequencing and duration. Finally, you'd hold a fourth meeting to review in detail the schedule produced based on the three previous meetings. Having four separate meetings gives the team time to ponder the project requirements and bring additional accuracy to the deliverable of each succeeding meeting. However, what often happens is that you only have time to hold one meeting with the team to extract all the necessary information to create the project schedule. It's the PM's job to collect all the information, sort it, place it in the correct documents, and make sure the documents correctly reflect all the project tasks and their relationships.

Scheduling Programs or Spreadsheets

Scheduling programs are wonderful tools for PMs. Many scheduling software packages are on the market today, including scheduling options in Visio and Lotus Notes. However, the one you're most likely to use is MS Project. MS Project allows you to easily enter tasks and enables you to play "what if?" games for projects. "What if" scheduling games are options in scheduling programs that give the PM the ability to see the impact to the project if there's a change of resources or change in sequencing of work packages.

TABLE 6.1: Scheduling Spreadsheet Sample

TASK #	TASK	DURATION	START DATE	END DATE	RESOURCE
1.1	Landscape Designed	5 days	1-Jan	5-Jan	Jim
1.2.1	Sprinkler Installed	10 days	6-Jan	15-Jan	Jim
1.2.2	Fertilizer Spread	2 days	16-Jan	17-Jan	Kevin
1.2.3	Sod Laid	7 days	18-Jan	24-Jan	Jim
1.2.4	Ground Leveled	2 days	25-Jan	26-Jan	Fred
1.3	Foliage Planted	7 days	27-Jan	2-Feb	Jim

Let's Schedule Overtime for the Duration of the Project

One way to minimize short-term resource stress on a project is to schedule personnel to work overtime. Keep in mind that many studies have shown that a work schedule of sixty hours or more per week that continues for more than two months results in the same productivity levels as if the employees worked only forty hours per week. In addition, overtime can result in increased absenteeism and a higher rate of employee injuries. Therefore, use overtime judicially to relieve resource availability issues.

Is There a Welder in the House?

Once I had to manage a plant outage. The project downtime was fourteen weeks. The baseline schedule showed that the duration of completing all the necessary repairs would take seventeen weeks. The PM used MS Project features to identify that if we could find two additional welders, we could cut the outage to thirteen weeks. That information is the type of information a PM can use to obtain additional resources for a project.

The new web management scheduling tools enable the entire teams to have easy access to the status of the project, review the pending task lists, and provide an easy process to report task status. Common examples for web-based scheduling software are Niku, RPM, and Primavera. Even with all these tools, I'm amazed at how often PMs choose to manage their projects with simple spreadsheets (see Table 6.1 on the previous page). Why do they use spreadsheets and not the fancy tools? Well, it works—spreadsheets are simple to keep up-to-date and can reflect exactly what the sponsor wants to see. The downside is that spreadsheets don't automatically calculate various scheduling functions or generate intricate reports. The upside is that almost everyone can read and manipulate the spreadsheet data to fit their own needs, and everyone has the necessary software on his or her desktop. Your company culture, your sponsor's preference, and your own judgment will determine which method you choose to use to manage each project.

Scheduling Reports

The output of schedule creation software is task status in some form of schedule. You can choose to display the schedule in Gantt charts, calendar formats, or spreadsheets, depending on your preference. Gantt charts *display* planned and actual progress for project tasks shown against a horizontal timeline. Gantt chart schedules can also display the project task interdependencies and task status. This format enhances a PM's ability to continually evaluate and update the schedule. Usually, scheduling software also allows you to create summary and milestone reports with minimum effort. Calendars are a familiar easy-to-read format. However, calendar schedules are good for a high-level view of simple projects and not good for task details. Spreadsheets are good for detailed task references but don't automatically calculate critical paths.

Keeping the Critical Path Visible

The best way to help the project team manage the critical path is to keep all critical path deliverables and their status visible. Listing the next critical path deliverable in bold at the top of your status report or posting it in a team meeting can keep the team focused on the completing the critical path tasks. If you have any indication that the date may slip, quickly get your team together to brainstorm options to keep the task on track.

Case Study

Patricia had the approved budget and used the sticky notes from the WBS to create the network diagram. The team took about an hour and placed the tasks in sequence. No additional tasks were identified during this process, so there was no need to revise the scope or WBS documentation.

TO SHARE OR NOT TO SHARE

I was told once you should never show a Gantt chart schedule to a manager. Schedules are tools only for the PM and team. I thought that was the most ridiculous thing I had ever heard. Then I reflected on other projects I completed. I realized that I spent hours and hours explaining to management how to read the Gantt chart schedule and trying to convince them to use it as a management tool. I was successful in getting management to use schedules only in extremely technical industries. I wanted to be efficient and maintain only one format. However, there's a conflicting demand for the schedule; most managers want a one-page executive summary that describes how the project is progressing, but PMs need considerably more scheduling detail to manage and track progress. Now I check with the project sponsor and identify what format will give them the appropriate level of meaningful information.

Patricia then entered the network diagram into the company-approved scheduling software. She used the level 1 deliverables as the summary items in the schedule, and then she used the level 2 deliverables identified in the WBS as milestones. Once she entered all the estimates, she checked to make sure the dates were what she expected, the summary report reflected the first level of the WBS, and the milestone report matched the second level from the WBS. As she expected, executing the contract and purchasing the hardware for configuration take thirty-two weeks each, which makes them both the critical path, followed closely by printing the nine user guides, currently scheduled for thirty weeks. She saved the schedule as the baseline schedule (see Figure 6.10).

Then she began to run some "what if?" scenarios to see if she could compress the schedule. She carefully looked at the critical path to see if she could add more resources to any tasks in order to reduce the duration. She identified an option to reduce the duration for executing the contract. Each review iteration was scheduled for four weeks. She plans to reduce contract review iterations by one iteration, which would cut four weeks from the schedule. She's going to set up a meeting after each company has had one set of changes where all the decision makers are in the room at one time. It looks like that can cut four weeks from the current schedule (see Figure 6.11), which will take the contract off the critical path.

The next critical path is the hardware procurement. She has already initiated the purchase order; she will set up a meeting with the purchasing agent to see if they can compress the timeline. You can see the impact to the schedule if she could obtain the hardware four weeks early (see Figure 6.12).

If both the procurement and contract can be reduced by four weeks, the user guides become the critical path. Patricia is going to see if she can get additional help to shorten the proofreading duration for the user guide.

FIGURE 6.10: Summary schedule

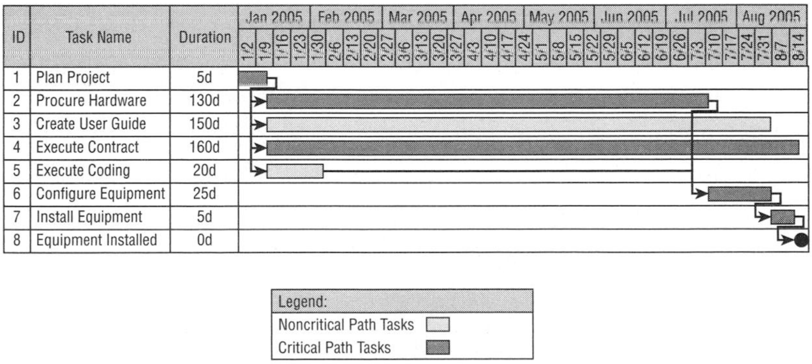

FIGURE 6.11: Summary schedule with critical path

ID	Task Name	Duration	Jan 2005	Feb 2005	Mar 2005	Apr 2005	May 2005	Jun 2005	Jul 2005	Aug 2005
1	Plan Project	5d								
2	Procure Hardware	130d								
3	Create User Guide	150d								
4	Execute Contract	140d								
5	Execute Coding	20d								
6	Configure Equipment	25d								
7	Install Equipment	5d								
8	Equipment Installed	0d								

Legend:
Noncritical Path Tasks
Critical Path Tasks

FIGURE 6.12: Potential project schedule based on reduced duration hardware procurement

ID	Task Name	Duration	Jan 2005	Feb 2005	Mar 2005	Apr 2005	May 2005	Jun 2005	Jul 2005	Aug 2005
1	Plan Project	5d								
2	Procure Hardware	110d								
3	Create User Guide	150d								
4	Execute Contract	140d								
5	Execute Coding	20d								
6	Configure Equipment	25d								
7	Install Equipment	5d								
8	Equipment Installed	0d								

Legend:
Noncritical Path Tasks
Critical Path Tasks

Patricia then met with Laurie to review the schedule. Laurie asked if the project could be done in 30 weeks because of a promise to the CEO. Patricia asked if there was something contingent on the completion of the project in 30 weeks or whether it was just a promised date. Laurie confessed it was a date she promised her boss. In addition, Laurie thought she could get extra help in the configuration portion of the project. Patricia explained the concept of the critical path to Laurie and explained she would continually manage the critical path to meet the finish date. Then she pointed out that the configuration tasks weren't on the critical path, and they had two weeks of float. The additional configuration help wouldn't reduce the duration of the project. Patricia showed Laurie that if they could get help to execute the contract with one fewer review iterations and if they could get the hardware four weeks earlier, the length of the project would be 30 weeks. Laurie agreed to support Patricia with her efforts to improve on the critical path tasks.

CHAPTER 7

Defining Your Quality Management Plan

Before the 1970s, the United States was known to have the highest-quality products in the world. In fact, customers accepted a certain number of defects for every product as long as the product performed the basic functions. During the 1970s, though, the definition of *quality* began to change. Customers began to increase their expectation from "it works" to "it must have the best design and superior support service." This trend was driven by other parts of the world changing their focus and giving customers what they wanted. Consequently, the United States' manufacturing reputation began to suffer because U.S. manufacturers continued to give customers what they always gave them, stuff that mostly worked. To compete with the rest of the world, the U.S. manufacturers had to adopt the *"customer first"* philosophy, which resulted in the corporate trend to integrate quality into everyday processes.

In addition, the customer service bar has been raised. Customers are smarter, and they now expect to speak to a real person for support 24/7, get their food the way they want it in less than 60 seconds, and interact with only happy, qualified people. This has increased a PM's responsibility because quality is now part of all projects, regardless of the size and impact. The challenge for PMs is that they must deliver products that meet or exceed customer expectations while managing to keep projects within the approved scope, schedule, and cost. This chapter will give you a high-level description of commonly used methods for managing and measuring the quality of projects and for incorporating quality into your project plan.

Implementing Quality Processes

Several popular quality systems are in use today, such as Total Quality Management (TQM) and Six Sigma (described in a moment). Any of them will work if the philosophy matches the culture of your company, and you have consistent, high-level commitment from top management. I know that some folks are smitten by one model or another and think their model is the only one that will work. However, I've worked in many industries, and each system will give a company the quality benefits the company is seeking as long as top management supports the value. In fact, I've found that all quality processes follow the same basic principles. All processes must be documented in order to standardize procedures so that the processes are predictable and repeatable. All process improvements are iterative and continuous and follow these steps: identify problems, analyze the problems, identify potential solutions, perform a cost-benefit analysis on solutions, implement a solution, measure the impact of the solution, and then adjust the process to implement the next level of improvements. Problem solving is based on facts, and the ultimate purpose is to focus on preventing problems.

Many industries have specific quality models that have been adopted and modified to match the industry-specific terminology and needs. These are defined either by regulation or by industry best practices. For example, the Federal Drug Administration mandates minimum quality processes for food, cosmetic, medical device, and pharmaceutical companies. All PMs should familiarize themselves with the basic quality concepts used in their industry and in their company. Many of these models seem to overlap, and some have been built on the foundations of other models. The following sections will give you a high-level overview of several common quality models.

International Organization of Standards (ISO)

During the 1940s, an international group of electronics experts got together to develop standards for manufacturing electronic equipment. The purpose was to provide a framework and common technological language to bridge the communication gap between suppliers and customers. The standardization concepts continued to expand across many industrial fields until today *International Oragnization of Standarization (ISO)* is the world's leading developer of standards. ISO is a voluntary, nongovernmental organization that comprises 146 countries. However, many countries and regulatory agencies mandate compliance with ISO standards.

The ISO 9000 series is the ISO quality standard. This is a framework for quality management that covers the processes for producing and delivering products and services for customers.

Total Quality Management (TQM)

The *Total Quality Management (TQM)* movement was started by the Japanese in the 1950s. Dr. W. E. Deming was invited to present his views on the basics of statistical quality control to the Union of Japanese Scientists and Engineers. His presentation made such an impact on the group that his lectures became the impetus for the creation of the Japanese Total Quality Control movement. This movement revolutionized the quality standards for all manufacturing. The United States began to adopt these strategies in the 1980s and at that time changed the name to TQM.

TQM teaches that the company should first be based on sound products, create processes that put the customer first, and then manage by fact (use data to make decisions) for continual process improvement. Management must be willing to put in place quality processes and support continuous employee training for TQM to be successful in any organization.

Six Sigma

General Electric first began using Six Sigma in 1995 after Motorola blazed the Six Sigma trail. *Six Sigma* uses data and statistical tools to identify ways to improve processes. Once the processes are improved, the procedures are documented to maintain those improvements in order to achieve the highest level of customer satisfaction. The Six Sigma metrics are always developed to align with company objectives and goals and are driven by a statistical representation of how a process is performing. By definition, a

Six Sigma process doesn't produce more than 3.4 defects per million opportunities. A defect is defined as anything outside customer specifications.
The basic Six Sigma process is DMAIC, which stands for the following:

- Define

- Measure

- Analyze

- Improve

- Control

Capability Maturity Model (CMM)

The Software Engineering Institute developed the*Capability Maturity Model
(CMM)* with assistance from MITRE corporations. This was an effort
to incorporate actual business best practices, TQM, and ISO standards to
improve software development processes. The basic CMM process is
to identify, isolate, investigate, innovate, count results, and revise processes
accordingly. CMM measures the maturity of the software development
process for a company from level 1 (few repeatable processes) to level 5 (all
processes documented, verified, and tested). A rough comparison between
ISO and CMM is that if your company complies with ISO 9001, you'll most
likely be able to meet CMM level 2 requirements.

NOTE   For more detail about these quality processes, you can visit the following websites: www.iso.org for ISO, www.isixsigma.com for Six
Sigma, www. Deming.org for TQM, and www.sei.cmu.edu/cmm
for CMM.

Using Quality Resources

PMs are jacks of all trades. They must be able to facilitate meetings, document projects, and identify and resolve issues, all while improving company processes. In addition, PMs must be able to identify when a

facilitated root-cause meeting should be held and when a procedure should be written. You can use the following tools to help you identify, validate, and resolve process issues and maintain quality in your projects.

Quality Department

The first question you need to answer is, does your company have a quality department? This is the department that defines the company quality objectives and processes and may also be responsible for product testing or auditing. If the answer to that question is "yes," then much of the quality management plan for your project may already be defined and documented. The quality department may use ISO, CMM, Six Sigma, or a company-specific model for quality management. Make sure your quality management plan supports any company quality objectives or values that are in place. PM needs a working knowledge of the corporate quality processes and procedures. This is an area you should request training in if you aren't comfortable with the standards or procedures.

If your company doesn't have a formal quality department, then your team needs to define the methods they'll use to maintain quality, including developing testing procedures and acceptance criteria for the project deliverables. You'll need to include the templates for the test plan, test scripts, and closeout test summaries as part of the project deliverables.

Quality Measurement

Your project team needs to identify what you're going to measure to ensure quality. Many common quality measurements exist: errors, bugs, defects per deliverable, cost per employee, or improved efficiency. If the team can set interim quality measurements, in addition to ones for the final product, you'll increase your chances of meeting customer expectations. For example, you may schedule beta tests (small prelaunch meetings with selected customers). These customers can identify necessary changes prior to the final launch of the product with a general release. For example, you could send enrollment software to a small group of customers to test the functionality. These customers can give you feedback on the product's usability. The project team can then evaluate the feedback and roll these suggestions into the product before the software is boxed and sold to the public. If your team uses beta releases, make sure this time is allotted for in the project plan and define how the team will select features to add to the product that are within the project scope.

Keep the team focused on whatever you've chosen to measure by keeping the goals and results visible. You can do this with charts on a wall or through status reports that highlight goals. While we all know we want a defect-free product, we need to continually inspect deliverables to ensure this. The techniques to inspect and measure deliverables is another improvement the quality revolution has given us. For example, we measure bugs per lines of code developed, the percent availability for manufacturing equipment, and the number of times a phone rings before customer service answers the call.

Quality Process Tools

You can employ many tools to improve processes and increase quality. Learning to use the following tools will help you identify and resolve at least 80 percent of the quality or process issues that you'll identify during your project. However, every PM will most likely use only a few of these tools depending on their industry or the types of projects they manage. Each of these tools requires at least a full chapter to describe the details of how to implement the technique; this is merely a high-level overview of the tools. Almost any book on ISO, TQM, Six Sigma, or CMM gives a detailed explanation of the following tools.

Graphs   You can use *graphs* (also known as run charts), shown in Figure 7.1, to spot trends in the data. They're also great to track trends that have a goal. To use this tool to collect data, determine the vertical and horizontal axes and plot the data. Make sure you have a clear-to-read graph that has horizontal labels, vertical labels, the source of the data, the date of graph creation (including the year), and a clear title.

FIGURE 7.1: Graph

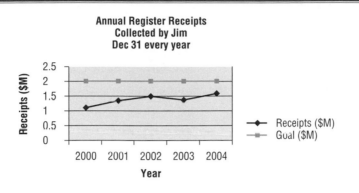

Flow charts *Flow charts*, shown in Figure 7.2, are the best tool to show the steps in a process and a foundation for procedures. From cleaning your house to building a nuclear power plant, flow charts are an easy way to show what action happens next. The process is to identify and document every step and decision point in a process. Once you document your process, you can use a flow chart to show redundant steps or illogical flows in a process. If you can't describe a process in a flow chart, I suspect you have a cumbersome, inefficient process.

Check sheets You can use *check sheets*, shown in Figure 7.3, to count. The trick with this tool is to identify what you'll count. To use this tool, you need to think through the output before you begin to collect data, or you'll have to go back and get the additional information later. For example, let's say you're going to count types of injuries at a manufacturing plant. After you put the charts together, someone asks what the ages of the people are by injury type. If you hadn't planned for collecting that data up front, you'll have to go back to get the people's ages.

Pareto Vilfredo Pareto defined the Pareto diagram, shown in Figure 7.4, in 1897. As an Italian economist, he found that using bar charts (also known as *histograms*) allows the user to identify potential reasons for problems based on fact. He's most famous for the identification of the 80-20 rule, which says that 20 percent of the items covers 80 percent of issues. This applies almost everywhere: 20 percent of your customers may provide 80 percent of the revenue, 20 percent of your team takes up 80 percent of your time, and 20 percent of your processes are going to cause 80 percent of your headaches. Pareto diagrams are great tools that can help identify where to focus efforts to make the biggest impact by allowing you to identify the big problem that could result in the largest improvement.

FIGURE 7.2: Flow chart

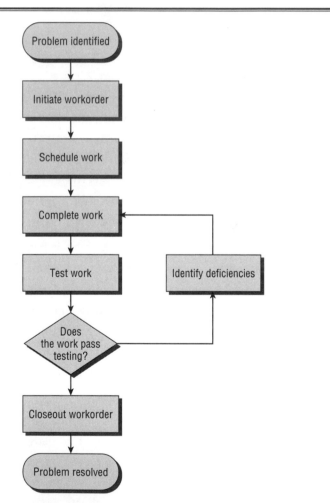

FIGURE 7.3: Check sheet

Injuries per Year

Age/Injury	Arm	Shoulder	Wrist	Leg	Knee	Ankle	Back	Total
20-30	■	■	■	▌	■	▌	▌	21
30-40	■	■	▌	▌	■	▌	■	28
40-50	▌	▌	■	▌	■	▌	■	23
50-60	▌	▌	■	▌	■	■	■	36
60-70	▌	▌	■	▌	■	▌	■	29
Total	15	17	20	6	37	14	28	

FIGURE 7.4: Pareto diagram

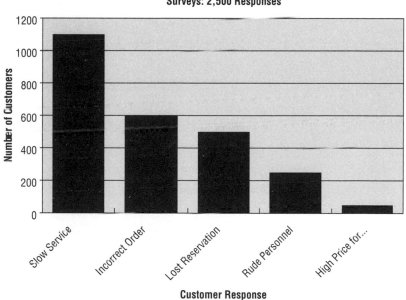

Restaurant Customer Responses Based on Table Surveys: 2,500 Responses

---

REDUCING EMPLOYEES TO ZERO

Our management team was in the process of creating the annual budget. Part of that exercise is always answering the question, How can we cut expenses? We were getting pressure from corporate to reduce the number of personnel. The team created a Pareto diagram for the makeup of our expense dollars. The big bar was material costs, and one of the small bars was personnel. As a joke, one of the team members ran the numbers of the impact if we got rid of all the people. The improvement was only 1 penny. If we could renegotiate the material contracts, we could easily cut our costs by 50 percent. Using this diagram, we were able to convince senior management that it was better to focus on renegotiating the material contracts rather than cutting personnel.

Fishbone analysis diagrams (Ishikawa diagrams) *Fishbone analysis diagrams* (also known as *Ishikawa diagrams* or *cause-and-effect diagrams*), shown in Figure 7.5, are great tools to drill down to find a problem's root cause. This is a tool that requires practice to use effectively, so don't get discouraged if the first few tries seem rough. To use this tool, you need to bring together a team of subject experts in a facilitated session to drill down through a cause-and-effect process to identify a problem's true root causes. This process is valuable because people often jump to conclusions and solutions when problems arise. When you see the same problem reoccurring, it's time to implement a root-cause analysis process because this is a prime indicator that the solution isn't the root cause but just a Band-Aid for a quick fix. The crucial part of this process is then to drill down and ask "why?" five times to each contributing cause of a problem to identify the real root causes.

FIGURE 7.5: Fishbone analysis diagram

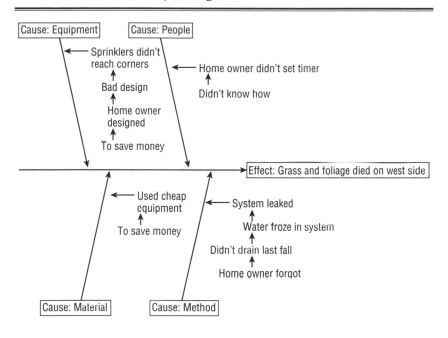

NOTE The crucial part of a root cause analysis process is to ask "why?" to each contributing cause to identify the real root causes. For example, the problem is that the lawn died. Why? It didn't get enough water. Why? The sprinkler system design didn't have water go to the corners of the yard. Why? The homeowner designed the sprinkler system. Why? The homeowner wanted to save money on the system. Why? The homeowner was selling the house. If you have a group that can't answer the "whys?" five deep, you probably have a team that's too high in the organization that can't give the detail you need to determine the root cause.

Procedures Procedures are tools that define processes. These documents are critical, as they are what the auditors will use to check your processes. I find that smaller projects give you the opportunity to document critical processes while you complete the project. If "continuous business process improvement" is a company value, then you can use procedures to identify and document process improvements. Every quality model requires procedures to document all essential processes. Use your process flow as the foundation of the procedure document. See Appendix B for the Project Procedure template.

Audits

Many people begin to quake when they're informed their group will be audited. I view auditors as my friends. They help identify problems, which are areas that can be improved. They can help you get management to understand the importance of procedures and processes and ultimately project management methodologies. Just remember these auditing rules:

- Rule 1: Auditors will make sure you're doing what you said you were going to do. Your first procedures need to document what you do, not what you wish the company would do. During your project, you can implement incremental improvements to the process. After all, most major improvement comes from the cumulative effect of many small improvements.

- Rule 2: If it wasn't written down, it never happened. You must be able to show that you had status meetings, who attended, and what was decided. If an approval was given verbally, it never happened. You must be able to show to whom and when the approval was given. If the approval was given in an e-mail, save the e-mail in the project folder.

The PM needs to describe in the quality plan whether the project will be audited and to what level. In addition, the quality plan needs to identify whether the audit will be done by an external company or by an internal audit department. If you are going to be audited, ask yourself if this process has been audited before and what the results of the previous audit were. Auditors become rather cranky when an issue was identified in the last audit and shows up again the next year with no improvement.

Creating a Quality Management Plan

The purpose of the aforementioned items is to help you understand quality fundamentals so you can create your quality management plan. A PM needs to facilitate the quality discussion with the project team and then create the quality plan that will be incorporated into the project plan (see Appendix B for the Quality Management Plan template). Quality plans help teams perform better because they encourage the team members to examine the methods and processes they're using to complete their work packages.

Quality assurance Describe the company quality processes or team-specific procedures for this project. Include whether you'll send the deliverables through a quality assurance or quality control department prior to launching the product. Define the acceptable level of defects for the product, fitness for use, and conformance to requirements.

Scope verification Describe the process you'll use to verify scope. Will this be included in the test plans or scripts? How will scope changes be incorporated into the revised test plans? This may be as simple as including the scope statements in the testing process to ensure that the scope has been met. For example, one of the scope statements may be to provide an enrollment product that accepts international phone numbers. The testing plan will define a test to ensure international phone numbers are accepted as part of an enrollment.

Document acceptance criteria Define the document acceptance criteria. Identify when and who will review and approve the documents. Describe the version control process and the criteria for document completion. We all know that most documents go through many drafts before they can be considered complete. This portion of the quality management plan should describe when a document is considered complete. For example, the project plan is considered complete when the sponsor approves the document.

NOTE   Many documents are never considered complete, as they're living documents that change during a product's life. These living documents need to be identified as such in the project plan.

Work package acceptance criteria   Define the work package *acceptance criteria*. Identify who will review and approve the work packages and when. Describe the version control process and the criteria for work package completion. Make sure this definition describes when the work package is *done-done*. Done-done is when everyone that has anything to do with the work package has completed all the work associated with the work package. For example, if you're developing an enrollment feature for a new product, the developers may think the work package is done when they've finished coding. However, the work package still needs to be tested and launched on the website. The work package isn't done-done until the public has access to the feature on the website.

Disaster recovery and business continuity plan   Do you have a corporate disaster recovery plan or business continuity plan that your project needs to revise or that you need to have documented in your project plan? Remember that you'll need to add new clients to any business continuity plan. This may not be part of a traditional quality management plan; however, it's an issue that's raised in many quality processes.

Process improvements   Describe the process improvements that will occur during this project. List any procedure you'll need to revise. If you identify these process improvements as part of the project plan, you'll keep these in the back of your mind as your work through the project. This will help to minimize time you have to spend revising documents during the project's closeout phase.

Audits   Identify any audits that will be performed on the project. Define when the audits will be performed and by whom. Make sure audits are captured in the schedule. This is particularly useful if your company has annual audits that may impact resources for your project.

Case Study

Patricia's company is using CMM to improve its software development processes. The company hired an external company to perform a CMM review, and that company determined they're currently at a level 1. The company goal is to reach CMM level 2 by the end of the year. To facilitate this process, the company has created a team to oversee the improvement of company processes to meet the year-end goal. The only audits that will be done on this project will be in conjunction with the CMM project.

Patricia works for a division that has a quality assurance (QA) group that will be responsible for performing all testing for the project. Patricia met with the head of quality assurance, Jaymie, to brief her on the project. Jaymie has included this project into her resource plan and told Patricia that she will have her staff begin to write the test plan for the project.

Right now the only procedures that Patricia plans on writing pertain to the configuration and implementation of new customers. The next team meetings will include creating the configuration and implementation flow charts as the foundation for the procedures. Patricia plans to meet with the CMM team to make sure she uses the approved CMM procedure template for these procedures. She also needs to make sure her project follows the correct processes identified by the CMM team and external auditors.

The quality plan will include information collected from the CMM team, the QA testing plan, and standard company processes. This project is very visible and requires a low level of defects for implementation. The scope statement has been approved and will be used for the development of the QA test scripts. All documents require an e-mail approval by the project sponsor. The e-mail approvals will be saved in the project folder. Work packages will be reviewed and approved by the PM prior to sending the work package to QA for testing. The QA manager will approve the successful testing of the work package, and this approval will constitute completion.

This project won't cause a change to the company disaster recovery plan. However, each new customer will have to be added to the business continuity plan. At this time, no additional process improvements need to be made during this project. Patricia told Laurie, the project sponsor, that she will escalate any potential process improvements as they're identified during the project.

CHAPTER 8

Defining the Procurement
Management Plan

So far I've gone over how to create a scope statement, select a team, manage risk, estimate tasks, create a budget, develop a schedule, and create a quality plan. The final section of the project management plan is the procurement management plan. This is going to be a bit of a catchall chapter. First, I'll review procurement, which involves purchasing resources or materials from outside the performing organization. The performing organization is the company that is responsible for the project. Second, I'll discuss the legal reviews you may need to do for your project. Purchasing resources and legal reviews, if necessary, are lengthy processes that often become the critical path of projects. And for small-to-medium-sized projects, using either of these performing either of these tasks requires constant attention to keep the project on schedule.

Purchasing Goods and Services

Procurement is defined as the process of acquiring resources outside the performing organization. For PMs, this may be synonymous with a project's Request for Proposal (RFP) process. I won't spend a lot of time on the RFP process for two reasons. First, for smaller projects, you rarely have time to follow a formal RFP process. Second, most companies have formal RFP processes you must follow if you need to go through a bidding process. For this discussion, the term resources refers to both people and materials. Purchasing agents and contract administrators are critical SMEs for any project that requires purchasing resources. These are the people who specialize in obtaining resources and ensuring that all contract documents are complete. They don't need to be part of the project team but need to be identified early in the project and kept in the communication loop.

The first question you need to answer with regard to procurement is, Am I going to make or buy the necessary resources for the project? If you decide to make a product rather than purchase it, then you don't need to perform the procurement process.

When to Use Your Purchasing Department

Company policies define the processes to obtain any resources or services that will be purchased from outside the performing organization. Even in new companies, these procedures protect the company and ensure that all purchases meet the minimum acceptance criteria. These processes usually include standard documentation with approved boilerplate language. *Boilerplate language* is the legal language that's used in documents similar to each other and has a definite meaning in the same context. Procurement processes should define approval levels for purchasing resources and contract signature authority. These processes usually describe the conditions that require using an RFP process. In this chapter I'll use RFP for any bid process, including Request for Information (RFI) or Request for Quote (RFQ). My experience is that companies stick to using only one type of bid process.

Why do you have to go through purchasing? Why can't you just go to the corner store and get what you want? Purchasing agents are the people who are responsible for acquiring the materials and resources for a company. Their focus is to get the best price for the resources while meeting contract and bidding requirements for the company. These folks maintain the approved vendor lists and have the authority to override the list if you have only a single source. They're also responsible for making sure the company follows state and federal contract purchasing rules, legal regulations, and any contractual commitments. Sometimes purchasing departments have exclusive contracts with vendors they must use as suppliers for certain merchandise.

ORDER EARLY

A few years ago I inherited a project from an engineer who had just completed the project planning. All I had to do was to manage the development, testing, and implementation of a product for a new customer. I reviewed all the planning and engineering documentation. The analysis and design documents were great, the requirements were detailed, and the schedule was thorough. However, I noticed that several pieces of equipment still needed to be ordered, and I knew they had fairly long lead times. I didn't see any documentation that indicated the parts had been ordered or that the lead time had been identified in the schedule. I quickly spoke to the engineer, and he said he hadn't gotten to that task yet because he was pretty busy with the engineering for the project. As I suspected, that critical part had a 90-day lead time, which meant the project couldn't begin for 90 days. We expedited ordering the part at a 100 percent markup and started the project 45 days behind schedule.

Typical Purchasing Flow

The following are the typical steps necessary to obtain resources for projects. If you're getting contractor resources, you need to also refer to Chapter 4 because you may need to incorporate interviewing time into the project schedule.

1. Decide whether to make or buy.

2. Identify the need and approximate size of the purchase.

3. Obtain approval for the purchase.

4. Write a quote with the appropriate level of requirements.

5. Obtain bids.

6. Select a vendor.

7. Write and execute purchase documents.

8. Order parts/equipment.

9. Receive the parts.

The flow for the RFPs is similar to the flow listed in this section except that the process also includes posting the procurement documents, creating and implementing evaluation criteria, and selecting a vendor.

Types of Purchasing Agreements

Purchasing agents can use many types of purchasing documents. Each one is designed to get the necessary resources with the most efficient use of time while protecting the company.

Master agreements *Master agreements* are contracts with vendors that describe the relationship between the parties. These agreements are used for long-term relationships. Details for what will be purchased is usually in attached documents such as statements of work, purchase orders, or pricing addendums.

Purchase orders *Purchase orders* are usually documents used to purchase standard items from approved vendors. If there's no master agreement, the boilerplate for these documents can be rather extensive and written in teeny-tiny print on the back of the document. An example is the order form for office supplies.

Service agreements *Service agreements* are documents used to obtain services from approved vendors. Services on these documents are generally simple services that don't require extensive description of deliverables with milestones and specific skills. An example is to create a service order to have snow removed from the parking lot this weekend.

RFPs *RFPs* are used when you need more detail in the products or services provided by an outside firm. These are used for more complex projects where the project team members don't have experience or are too busy to perform the task themselves. Often, RFP processes are used when the cost of the material or services exceeds a certain amount, when the services extend for a certain period, or by law when you're working for a government agency. The standard bid process includes creating a procurement plan, creating a solicitation plan, soliciting requests for bids, selecting a vendor, and completing the contract and contract close-out.

NOTE You can think of the *P* in RFP as an indicator of a problem, and you're searching for a solution. Hence, the proposal should specify a solution to a problem and is judged on more than price and delivery.

Purchasing Requirements

Two trains of thought exist for how much detail is needed for project requirements. One is to give detailed requirements to get exactly what you need. The other is to give broad requirements in order to give vendors the opportunity to present new-and-improved solutions. You'll need to decide which is better for each project as the procurement management plan is created. The common complaint I hear about purchasing departments is that they select only the lowest bidder, which doesn't always meet the project's needs. Sometimes that happens when the PM didn't clearly state requirements; sometimes, you have no choice but to go with the lowest bidder.

Now is the time to define the purchasing requirements using the Procurement Management Plan template (see Appendix B for this template). You're still in the planning portion of the project, so you may need to revise this information as you work on the project. List the probable vendor, item description, expected lead time, delivery date, and estimated cost.

Many master agreements allow for partial payments based on partial delivery of materials or resources. It's up to the PM to define project milestones that can be used to trigger these payments. Make sure these milestones are specific enough to know that the milestone has in fact been reached in order to avoid spending time proving that the milestone was completed. For example, in the landscaping project, payment milestones might be after the sprinkler system passes the pressure test, after the sod is laid and rolled, and finally after all the shrubs are planted.

Knowing When Should You Use an Attorney

As with the purchasing department, using the legal department is critical for the success of many projects. A PM needs the services of an attorney while managing a project in two conditions. The first is for negotiating legal documents such as contracts. The second is for guidance for intellectual property. *Intellectual property* is the legal field that comprises trademarks, service marks, copyrights, and patents. Intellectual property management is often not discussed in descriptions of project management plans. However, the care and use of company branding is part of every employee's job.

Contract Attorneys

The contract attorney's role is to assist you in negotiating and executing any agreement between parties. Attorneys are trained to identify and eliminate all risk for the company they represent. But eliminating all risk isn't always possible. You must understand that any agreement between parties has risks, and the purpose of negotiating the agreement is actually to balance the risks. Your role, as the PM, is to identify how much risk you and the company are willing to take to enter into this agreement. A good contract describes a mutually beneficial agreement with balanced risks.

Contract Types

Many types of legal agreements exist. Usually, the primary agreement is a contract or master agreement. The legal definition of a *contact* is an agreement between two or more persons that creates an obligation to do or not to do a particular thing in exchange for something of value, usually money. Let your attorney make sure you've created an appropriate legal agreement. Your role is to review and ensure that any dates or amounts are correct. These are the easiest things to measure to ensure you've complied with the agreement. Review the contract dissolution sections to make sure you're aware of what can cause the contract to be breached. Also, review the liability and damages sections to make sure they're reasonable. Once a contract is executed, all times listed in the document and all other corresponding legal documents create an enforceable obligation.

Most people don't understand that many other documents are incorporated by reference into the contract. For example, I've seen people answer RFPs to get the bid, not intending to supply the deliverables described in the RFP response. RFPs, SOWs, and addendum documents are all part of the contract and are enforceable as such. Not complying with said documentation could be used as evidence for breach of contract. Breach of contract is a failure to perform any promise that's part of the contract; it can result in damages and the dissolution of the contract.

You can use three major types of contracts to document the relationship between parties for a project. All of them have pros and cons, and you should evaluate each with regard to the intent of the project.

Fixed-price contract A *fixed-price contract* is a type of contract in which the buyer agrees to pay the seller a definite, predetermined price. The risk increases for both parties if the deliverables aren't well defined because the buyer may not receive the expected product and the seller must bear the additional costs of work. You can add incentives, such as bonuses, to the contract to increase the seller's motivation for meeting or exceeding the contract objectives.

Cost-reimbursable contract A *cost-reimbursable contract* is a type of contract in which the buyer reimburses the seller for their actual costs plus a fee for the seller's profit. Costs include both direct costs (costs associated with the project) and indirect costs (overhead). The buyer incurs most of the risk with this type of contract, as the total cost is unknown.

Time and material contract A *time and material contract* is a type of contract that contains features of both the fixed-price contract and the cost-reimbursable contracts. These are used for smaller, short-term contracts when there isn't a well-defined scope for the deliverables. The fixed portion refers to the rate at which resources will be paid (either a per-hour rate or a per-item amount). The risk with this type of contract is that scope can grow out of control if the buyer doesn't manage it carefully.

Typical Flow and Timeline for Legal Processes

I usually schedule 12 weeks for contract negotiation for smaller projects. Many project sponsors have argued that the current is a critical project and that they're sure these negotiations will go more quickly and smoothly than my previous projects. Invariably, we're pushing for final signatures around week 12. The following steps are the typical set of tasks required for contract negotiation and execution; you can use them as a baseline in your project schedule:

1. Obtain the internal sample document: one week.

2. Revise the contract language: two weeks.

3. Sponsor an attorney review: two weeks.

4. Review and revise the contract with the PM, sponsor, and attorney: two weeks.

5. Review and revise the internal contract version, including walking through with both parties (scheduling this meeting is usually the tough part): two weeks.

6. Review and revise the contract with the PM, sponsor, and attorney: one week.

7. Execute the contract: one week.

NOTE If you can get all the right parties in one room after the initial review session, you can reduce weeks in the negotiation process. Make sure you have the decision makers in the meeting, or you will still have the review and approval cycles to go through and you won't be able to reduce the duration of the task.

Protecting Intellectual Property

One of the overlooked areas for the project management plan is the strategy to protect corporate intellectual property. While your project may not need additional trademarks or copyrights, you could inadvertently invalidate corporate endeavors to protect other intellectual property. The PM must not only be aware of the importance of following company direction in these areas but also be an advocate to the project team for these processes.

Patent and trademark attorneys are different from contract attorneys. Contract attorneys may not even think to ask about the intellectual property other than to include the boilerplate language in their standard contracts. Make sure the contracts identify who owns the intellectual property when the project is completed.

Using patent attorneys is becoming even more important in this age of new technology. Company branding is revised and posted on websites almost daily. It's the PM's responsibility to be aware of the necessity to get the patent attorney's approval prior to launching websites or publishing documents.

NOTE   Make sure you've executed Nondisclosure Agreements (NDAs) before you share company secrets with your vendors; otherwise, the information becomes public property, and anyone can use it.

A *patent portfolio* is a collection of patents that build upon one another, which ends up creating a niche for a company. If your company is one that's building its patent portfolio, make sure your product is either something that should be patented or something that doesn't violate a current patent.

Branding includes the look and feel, trademark, service marks, company names, logos, and any tag lines associated with these marks. Branding has become a major item in company goodwill and is considered a valuable asset. Companies spend millions of dollars creating brand image and must take care to use their branding consistently. If you're using a company brand, make sure you use it exactly as specified, or you may be risking the company's ability to register and maintain that brand. This is the reason marketing departments make sure all company collateral is reviewed by their legal department prior to publishing any documentation. If another company can show that you don't use the branding consistently, they can use that information as evidence that the company doesn't intend to seriously manage the brand, which means that company runs the risk of losing it.

Copyright laws change all the time, particularly with increasing development in technology. Copyrights are the legal rights to use literary property as granted to the author. It used to be that you obtained a copyright only if you sent in the document with the date and obtained an official copyright from the federal Patent Trademark Office. Now, the standard is that you need to carefully track the document, dates, and changes in order to demonstrate you were in control of the document and the language during the dates identified. Copyright challenges become an issue only if another company claims you used its copyrighted material. These lawsuits are expensive for both parties and should be avoided.

Case Study

Volte has an experienced purchasing department with well-documented procedures. Patricia identified early in the project that there was a need to order equipment. She has already met with the purchasing agent, Marybeth, and began the ordering process to order standard, off-the-shelf equipment. This is a small project that doesn't require any quotes or bids for equipment, and the work is all being done in-house, so it doesn't need contract labor. Further, no partial payment milestones are necessary for this project.

This project requires a new contract with Brown Enterprises. Patricia has already received a copy of the standard contract from Sharyl Kay, the Volte attorney, and is in the process of revising the language with the project sponsor. Going through the procurement management plan, Patricia was reminded that she needed to get signed NDAs from Brown Enterprises. She sent the standard NDA to Michele, Brown Enterprise's PM, this morning.

Volte doesn't spend much time or money on patents, which means this project has no patent issues.

Branding is going to be a bigger issue with this project. The new product implementation will carry dual branding from both Volte and Brown Enterprises. The user guides will need to be revised to include Volte branding and the schedule needs new dates to incorporate the user guides' new language. No other changes are planned for the user guides.

The procurement management plan is the final document required for the project management plan. Now that Patricia has completed the project management plan, it's time to review it with Laurie, the sponsor, and schedule the project kickoff meeting. The next chapter will explain how to prepare for the kickoff meeting and the recommended agenda.

CHAPTER 9

Formalizing the Plan

You've created the project plan document. Various members of the project team helped create most of the document. The project sponsor has reviewed the entire project plan and given final approved for it, including all the associated documentation. Now is the time to present the final version in a formal forum to all the project stakeholders. This meeting, called the *project plan kickoff meeting*, can be as dramatic or mundane as you want to be. However, this is the time where all the stakeholders need to understand not only the description of the project but also the detailed plan for completing the project tasks. The PM must create an atmosphere where all the participants are both physically and mentally engaged during the meeting. Everyone's participation is imperative so you can establish a solid foundation of understanding for successfully completing the project. This chapter discusses how to get the most out of the project plan kickoff meeting.

Creating the Project Kickoff Meeting Agenda

The purpose of the project plan kickoff meeting is to review the project plan and obtain final, formal approval from the stakeholders. You've already been meeting with many members of the project team to create the scope statement, risk response plan, budgets, and schedules. You've already gotten sponsor approval for the scope, budget, and schedule. However, the project plan kickoff meeting is when all the stakeholders understand and agree on the approach for all aspects of the project. This is also a time when you need to set the tone, tempo, and format for all future project meetings. To start, the PM should create and distribute meeting agendas with either the project documents or the location of the project documents at least 48 hours in advance.

The project plan kickoff meeting is probably going to be one of the longest meetings you'll schedule for this project. Make sure you don't cut the scheduled meeting time so short that you can't sufficiently review all the documentation. Schedule time in the agenda for discussions about technical or controversial aspects of the project. Assign approximate times and a presenter for each topic covered on the agenda (refer to Appendix B for the Project Plan Kickoff Agenda template).

It's next to impossible to facilitate a meeting and keep accurate notes while watching the meeting time. It's even more difficult if you have some antagonistic parties in the meeting. Make sure you've identified a scribe and timekeeper for the meeting. You'll have a lot of information to cover in this meeting, and you need to stay on track.

Remember, the project plan is the document that describes how the project will be managed. In preparing for the kickoff meeting, the PM should take this opportunity to review and update project plan documents. Keep in mind that many of the documents created for the project plan are living documents that may change throughout the project life cycle. For example, the project schedule will continue to grow and change throughout the project. The project stakeholders will want to review the most up-to-date versions of these documents in the kickoff meeting.

The project plan document will include all the documents created in Chapters 2 through 8. The following is a checklist of the documents that need to be part of the project plan (see Appendix B for templates).

- Project scope statement (Chapter 2)
- Risk management plan (Chapter 3)
- Risk response plan (Chapter 3)
- Team selection template (Chapter 4)
- Communication management plan (Chapter 4)
- Task analysis sheets (Chapter 5)
- Budget spreadsheet (Chapter 5)

- Baseline schedule (Chapter 6)

- Quality plan template (Chapter 7)

- Procedures template (Chapter 7)

- Procurement management plan (Chapter 8)

Do You Have to Make a Project Plan?

I've found that detailed project planning will contribute more to the ultimate success of a project and will allow you to minimize the time you'll need to spend on executing and managing the project. Walking through the entire plan with the project team and getting agreement on the outcome puts the information in everyone's heads. Subconsciously everyone continues to work toward the agreed upon outcome regardless of the distractions put in front of the project team.

For example, I started a software product development project that was originally determined to be high profile. I developed a thorough project plan and obtained stakeholder approval of the project plan. Two months later the project sponsor left the company. A month after that, a corporate reorganization moved most of the stakeholders to another division. The core project team was left intact, but the priority of the project was reduced to "do it in your spare time." Only a few project meetings took place, and no formal schedule was maintained. A year later, management decided they didn't want to put more time or money into the project. We performed a formal project closeout to determine the status of the product. Unbelievably, most of the project goals were met, and the deliverables met the expectations identified by the scope statement. Time and again, in projects that feel like they've gone out of control, I've found that if a good project plan is in place, the project has a much greater chance to meet the stakeholder expectations than projects that jump straight into execution.

Facilitating the Kickoff Meeting

The purpose of this meeting is to ensure that all project stakeholders agree on the project direction and to bridge the gap from project planning to project execution and control. At this point in the project, the volume of the project documents may be a bit overwhelming to many of the stakeholders. This means you'll need to define the appropriate level of detail to present at the meeting so the stakeholders understand the project. You don't need to review all the identified risks or the detailed requirements to have the stakeholders understand the project plan.

Use a variety of communication tools to convey the information, such as charts, PowerPoint presentations, and plain-old handouts. This may be a bit obvious, but please don't read the documents to the stakeholders. This is tempting when many of the participants haven't read the documentation prior to attending the meeting. But the people who come to the meeting prepared will "tune out" just like children at nap time.

The following are the expected outcomes for each agenda item; use this list as a guideline for covering the correct project plan details:

Meeting start This is the introduction for the meeting where the PM reviews the agenda, schedules meeting breaks, identifies the method for collecting issues, and handles any other meeting administrative information.

Expected outcome: To start the meeting on time and identify the purpose of the meeting.

Team introductions You can introduce each member individually or through an icebreaker exercise.

Expected outcome: To get the project team through the forming stage of team development. Creating an opportunity for each attendee to speak early in the meeting will enhance meeting participation.

Scope statement review This portion of the meeting is to review the project scope statement, including objectives, justification, team goals, project goals, critical success factors, assumptions, and deliverables.

The PM will have to decide how detailed this review should be based on participation in the original creation of the document. This is also the place where the PM and project team review the scope management process for all the stakeholders.

Expected Outcome: To obtain stakeholder agreement on the scope statement of the project. To ensure that the stakeholders understand the scope management process for project change requests.

Risk management plan review You'll review the risk management plan and the process for identifying and evaluating project risks. This should be a standard company process so that this is a quick review.

Expected outcome: To get the stakeholders to understand the process for risk identification and scoring. To get the stakeholders to understand the importance of identifying risks early in the project and to know the process to raise new risks. The final outcome is to obtain agreement on the risk management plan and process.

Risk analysis review The risk response plan may be a rather extensive document that you may not want to review in detail at this meeting. Discuss the process used to define the risk response, triggers, and contingency plans for the high-risk issues.

Expected outcome: To get the stakeholders to agree with the risk response plan for the high-risk issues. To get the risk owners to understand their responsibility with regard to the risks they've been assigned.

Role and responsibility review The PM will review the project roles and responsibilities and obtain agreement from the project team and stakeholders.

Expected outcome: To get all project stakeholders to understand their roles, their responsibilities, and the corresponding impact to the project.

Communication management plan review The PM will facilitate a review of the communication management plan. This may include creating meeting rules or reviewing standard company meeting rules. Make sure you review the documents that will be used to manage this project, such as status reports and issue logs. Identify which project documents are static or living as well as the location and author of each document.

Expected outcome: To obtain agreement on the communication process, meeting rules, and escalation plan. Also to get the project team to agree on the frequency of communication and meeting schedule.

Budget review   The PM will describe the task analysis process for the project stakeholders, including how that information was used to create the budget. The review of the budget spreadsheet can be a high-level review of the key items and the final budget figures. Be prepared to discuss details if the stakeholders don't agree with the final figures.

Expected outcome: To get the stakeholders to agree on the project budget.

Schedule review   It isn't necessary to review the detailed schedule at this project kickoff meeting. A summary-level review of the schedule that identifies the milestones, deliverable dates, and critical path tasks will be sufficient to understand the project plan.

Expected outcome: To get the stakeholders to understand the project schedule at a summary level. The critical path tasks need to be clearly understood (as well as the impact to the project if these dates aren't met).

Quality plan review   The PM will review the quality plan for the project and any project reviews or audits that have been scheduled for this project. Review any procedures that have been identified for creating or revising the quality plan.

Expected outcome: To obtain agreement on the approach and processes to measure and ensure quality. To get stakeholder agreement on the procedure creation or revision process.

Procurement management plan review   The procurement management plan review will include a review of the processes for both purchasing and legal as they pertain to this project.

Expected outcome: To get stakeholder agreement on the purchasing and legal process for this project. To get the project team to understand the impact of missing any target dates for these tasks.

Approvals The scribe will document attendance at the meeting and open issues identified during the meeting. Remember that you need documented approvals to meet any project audit reviews.

Expected outcome: To get the project stakeholders to understand and approve the project plan. To get final formal approval signatures for the project plan (based on company policy).

You'll find the Project Plan Kickoff Agenda template in Appendix B.

CRITICAL PATH ASSIGNMENTS

In kickoff meetings, I clearly identify the critical paths. I also identify who is responsible for completing the critical path tasks. We discuss any triggers that initiate contingency plans associated with the critical path tasks. These tasks are always reviewed in every status meeting, and there's always pressure to complete the critical path tasks schedule. Team members responsible for critical path tasks are always visible. A reputation that includes the ability to continually complete critical tasks on time can be a boon to your career. If you're not able to complete on time, you aren't likely to progress in your career. You have to be in charge of critical path tasks. This is an informal way to keep the rest of the project tasks on schedule.

Case Study

Patricia has scheduled a four-hour project plan kickoff meeting for next Thursday from 8 A.M. to noon. She wanted to have the meeting early so everyone would be fresh. She has created the agenda and distributed it to the project stakeholders. All the project documents are on the LAN in the project folder, and Patricia has given the location to all meeting participants.

The corporate culture is one that's a bit lax with regard to starting and ending meetings. Patricia and Laurie would like to set a new expectation for this project, so Laurie has agreed to start the meeting at 8 A.M. sharp. Patricia is going to bring in bagels and fruit to the meeting, as she has found people tend to stay at meetings that have food. The agenda presentations are going to be given by the project team so the entire meeting isn't facilitated by only one person. This also gives the team members experience in facilitating meetings.

Volte has standard meeting rules posted in every conference room. Patricia has learned that people forget common meeting etiquette, so she's going to review the meeting rules as part of the administrative portion of the meeting initiation.

Since most of the project team has never worked together before, Patricia is going to use an icebreaker exercise where people are paired and given five minutes to learn an interesting fact about the other person. People are then asked to introduce their partner and share the interesting fact.

Patricia has decided to review the entire scope statement document in detail to make sure all the stakeholders understand all the assumptions and critical success factors for this project. None of the project requirements will be reviewed at this meeting, but the stakeholders will be directed to view them in the project folder.

The risk management plan is a standard Volte process. However, many of the stakeholders for this project are with Brown Enterprises, so Patricia plans to give a brief overview of the process. The project team has decided to review those risks that have been identified as "high probability" and "high impact" and develop the corresponding risk response plans.

The roles and responsibilities have been reviewed with most of the stakeholders prior to the project plan kickoff meeting, so this will be a quick review of the role and responsibility matrices from the team selection template.

Patricia will have a copy of all the task analyses for the project in case someone has questions. She plans to review only the high-level project budget during this meeting. The project budget has come in under the original stakeholder expectations, so she doesn't think there will be an issue with the budget.

The quality plan is another standard process for Volte. Brown Enterprises has concerns about the quality of the conversion and implementation, so Patricia is going to spend a few extra minutes discussing the details of the quality plan. The project will follow the standard corporate project review, which includes the mid-project and project closeout reviews, will be held during this project. The Volte implementation and conversion procedures are going to be reviewed and revised as part of this project.

Patricia is going to spend quite a bit of time on the procurement plan because both the hardware purchases and contract execution is on the critical path. Both Marybeth and Sheryl Kay, the task owners, are going to be at the project plan kickoff meeting.

Patricia has spent approximately 35 percent of the estimated project time on project planning. Her experience has shown that this is a good rule-of-thumb figure. The project team is excited about starting this project because the project has well-defined scope, processes, and boundaries, which the members helped to define. They think the project plan is reasonable and can be completed successfully. Laurie, the project sponsor, is enthusiastic about the project and has been extremely supportive of the time and effort it has taken to create the project plan. Patricia has to continue to fuel the enthusiasm of the team to manage the project to a successful completion.

Nine Knowledge Areas Refresher

$\mathbf{T}$his appendix is a crash course on *A Guide to the PMBOK*'s project management process groups and the nine knowledge areas. All projects progress through a logical series of steps, starting with the initiation of a project all the way through to the ending, or closing, of the project. The information in this appendix will describe each of these processes along with the types of results or outcomes you're likely to see from each.

Following the process groups discussion, you'll find the nine knowledge areas. These describe the types of information and knowledge project managers must have to successfully run projects. Each knowledge area lists the project management processes found within that discipline, according to the 2000 and 2004 versions of *A Guide to the PMBOK*. Every four years, the Project Management Institute (PMI) modifies and enhances *A Guide to the PMBOK*. Changes reflect new information, industry trends, and best practices. Since the Spotlight Series spans both the 2000 and 2004 versions, you'll find both process listings in this appendix.

Project Management Process Groups

A Guide to the PMBOK describes and organizes the work of a project into five process groups: Initiating, Planning, Executing, Monitoring and Controlling, and Closing. Each group is interrelated and depends on the other. For example, you can't start the work of the project (Executing) without first initiating the project and creating a project plan—unless, of course, you work in Information Technology (IT) where we like to program the new system before we ask for requirements and then wonder why the end user doesn't like what we've done. (I trust all you great project managers out there are changing this paradigm.)

These process groups are iterative, meaning you might make several passes through each one throughout the course of the project. For example, changes might occur as a result of measurements you've taken (during the Monitoring and Controlling process) that require you go back to the Planning process and rework the schedule of some other part of the project plan. Risk management is iterative as well and should be performed throughout the life of the project.

Initiating

Initiating is the beginning process for all projects. This is where you decide whether to undertake the project by examining the costs and benefits of the project to the organization. It may also include an analysis of one project versus another project. For example, should you research and market a new product or consolidate the offices so all employees work under one roof? In the end, the Initiating process results in one of two decisions for each project considered—go or no go. Provided the answer is go, resources are committed to the project.

NOTE   Initiation is the formal recognition that a project, or the next phase in an existing project, should begin.

Some of the results produced during the Initiating process include the following:

- Defining the goals and objectives of the project
- Evaluating and determining project benefits
- Selecting projects based on criteria defined by a selection committee
- Writing the project charter
- Assigning the project manager
- Obtaining sign-off of the project charter

Planning

The Planning processes are the heart of all successful projects. And proper planning techniques can be the difference between a failed project and a successful one. This process outlines what's involved in completing the work of the project, where you're going, and how you're going to get there. As you probably already know, this process can consume a large amount of the overall project time, but it's well worth the investment.

Project planning involves researching, communicating, and documenting—and lots of it. What you do here will determine how the project will progress through the remaining processes. It also establishes the foundation for the rest of the project. If you communicate well with the stakeholders through this process, assure that all project team members and stakeholders understand the purpose of the project and how the work will be carried out, and establish a professional decorum with everyone involved, the stakeholders will feel confident that the project will be successful. You're also more likely to gain their cooperation later in the project when the problems start to appear.

Some of the results produced during Planning include the following:

- Determining project deliverables and milestones
- Writing and publishing a scope statement
- Determining requirements
- Breaking down the work of the project into tasks and creating a Work Breakdown Structure (WBS)
- Developing a project schedule
- Establishing a project budget
- Developing risk, communication, quality, and change management plans
- Determining resource needs
- Assessing special skills needed for project tasks and identifying resources
- Setting the stage for project success

NOTE   The Planning group is the largest of all the process groups. The project plans created here are the road map for achieving the goals the project was undertaken to address.

Executing

While the Planning process is the heart of determining project success, the Executing process is where the real work of the project actually happens. Great plans require follow-through, and this is what you do in the Executing process group.

In the Executing process you'll put all the project plans you've developed into action. Project team members complete the tasks. You keep the project team focused on the work of the project, and you communicate project progress to stakeholders and management. Once the work of the project begins, sometimes you'll need to change the project plan. It's the project manager's responsibility to update the project planning documents and redirect and refocus the project team on the correct tasks.

The Executing process is where you'll likely utilize the majority of project resources, spend most of the project budget, and run into scheduling conflicts.

Some of the results produced during the Executing process include the following:

- Obtaining project resources
- Establishing the project team
- Directing and leading the project team
- Conducting project status meetings
- Publishing project status reports and other project information
- Communicating project information
- Managing and directing contractors
- Managing project progress
- Implementing quality assurance procedures

Monitoring and Controlling

This group of project management processes involves monitoring the work of the project and taking performance measures to assure that the work performed is on track with the project scope and that the deliverables are being met. If performance checks during this process show that the project has veered off course, corrective action is required to realign the work of the project with the project goals.

Corrections and changes during this process may require a trip back through the Planning and Executing processes. Most often this will occur for one of two reasons—change requests or corrective actions.

Some of the results produced during the Monitoring and Controlling process include the following:

- Measuring performance and comparing to project plan
- Ensuring that the project progresses according to plan
- Taking corrective action when measures are outside limits
- Evaluating the effectiveness of corrective actions
- Reviewing and implementing change requests
- Updating the project plan to conform with change requests

Closing

The Closing process is the one project managers tend to skip. Once the project at hand is complete, it's easy to start focusing on the next one. Who wants to obtain sign-off, document lessons learned, and close out a project that's complete and that stakeholders love? You should.

One of the most important aspects of this process is documenting lessons learned. You and your project team have just completed a successful project where some processes worked very well and others could have been improved. Now is the time to capture the good and the bad so that the next project you (or another project manager in your company) undertake capitalizes on the lessons learned during this project.

Another aspect of this process is celebrating. Your team has met or exceeded the agreed-upon project goals, and the stakeholders are satisfied. That spells success, and success should be celebrated. Projects are truly team efforts, and it's always appropriate to congratulate your team on a job well done.

Some of the results produced during the Closing process include the following:

- Obtaining acceptance of project deliverables

- Securing sign-off from all stakeholders

- Documenting lessons learned

- Archiving project records

- Formalizing the closure of the project

- Releasing project resources

Figure A.1 shows the interaction and iterative nature of these process groups. While all the process groups are iterative, you'll find that most interaction occurs between the Planning, Executing, and Controlling process groups.

FIGURE A.1: Project process groups

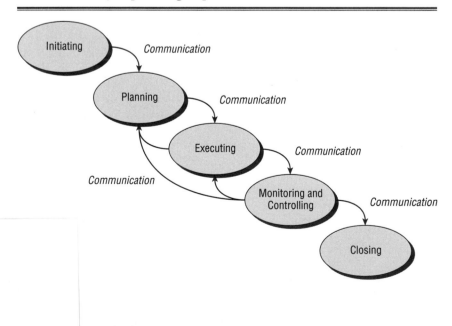

Project Management Knowledge Areas

According to *A Guide to the PMBOK*, nine knowledge areas comprise project management: Project Integration Management, Project Scope Management, Project Time Management, Project Cost Management, Project Quality Management, Project Human Resources Management, Project Communications Management, Project Risk Management, and Project Procurement Management. Each knowledge area deals with a specific aspect of project management such as scope management and time management. These areas consist of individual processes that have characteristics in common. For example, the Project Procurement Management knowledge area consists of processes dealing with procurement planning, solicitation, source selection, contract administration, and so on.

You should familiarize yourself with each knowledge area and the processes they include. They provide the foundation for solid project management practices.

If you'd like further information on these knowledge areas and their processes, pick up a copy of *PMP Project Management Professional Study Guide* by Kim Heldman.

The knowledge areas and a brief description of each follow.

Project Integration Management

The Project Integration Management knowledge area is concerned with coordinating all aspects of the project plan and is highly interactive. It involves project planning, project execution, and change control. All these processes occur throughout the life of the project and are repeated continuously while working on the project. Project planning, execution, and change control are tightly linked. The processes that constitute Project Integration Management include the following:

2000 PMBOK	2004 PMBOK
Project Plan Development	Develop Project Charter
Project Plan Execution	Develop Preliminary Project Scope

2000 PMBOK	2004 PMBOK
Integrated Change Control	Develop Project Management Plan
	Direct and Manage Project Execution
	Monitor and Control Project Work
	Integrated Change Control
	Close Project

Project Scope Management

The Project Scope Management knowledge area is concerned with defining all the work of the project and only the work required to complete the project. The processes involved in project scope management occur at least once during the life of the project and sometimes many times throughout the life of the project. For instance, Scope Planning entails defining and documenting the work of the project. Scope Change Control is the process that handles changes to the agreed-upon scope. Changes, as you probably guessed, require changes to the Scope Planning process, and thus the cycle perpetuates. The processes that constitute Project Scope Management include the following:

2000 PMBOK	2004 PMBOK
Initiation	Scope Planning
Scope Planning	Scope Definition
Scope Definition	Create WBS
Scope Verification	Scope Verification
Scope Change Control	Scope Control

Project Time Management

The Project Time Management knowledge area is concerned with setting the duration of the project plan activities, devising a project schedule, and monitoring and controlling deviations from the schedule. Time management is an important aspect of project management because it keeps the project activities on track and monitors those activities against the project plan to ensure the project is completed on time. The processes that constitute Project Time Management include the following:

2000 PMBOK	**2004 PMBOK**
Activity Definition	Activity Definition
Activity Sequencing	Activity Sequencing
Activity Duration Estimating	Activity Resource Estimating
Schedule Development	Activity Duration Estimating
Schedule Control	Schedule Development
	Schedule Control

Project Cost Management

As its name implies, the Project Cost Management knowledge area involves project costs and budgets. The activities in the Project Cost Management area establish estimates for costs and resources and keep watch over those costs to ensure that the project stays within the approved budget. The processes that make up Project Cost Management include the following:

2000 PMBOK	**2004 PMBOK**
Resource Planning	Cost Estimating
Cost Estimating	Cost Budgeting
Cost Budgeting	Cost Control
Cost Control	

Project Quality Management

Project Quality Management ensures that the project meets the requirements that the project was undertaken to produce. It focuses on product quality as well as the quality of the project management processes used during the project's life cycle. The processes in this knowledge area measure overall performance, monitor project results, and compare them to the quality standards. All this means the customer will receive the product or service they thought they purchased. The processes that constitute Project Quality Management include the following:

2000 PMBOK	2004 PMBOK
Quality Planning	Quality Planning
Quality Assurance	Perform Quality Assurance
Quality Control	Perform Quality Control

Project Human Resource Management

Ah, the people factor. Project activities don't perform themselves. It takes a village...no, that's someone else's line. It takes people to perform the activities of a project. The Project Human Resource Management knowledge area assures that the human resources assigned to the project are used in the most effective way possible. Some of the skills covered in this knowledge area include personal interaction, leading, coaching, conflict management, performance appraisals, and so on. The processes that constitute Project Human Resource Management include the following:

2000 PMBOK	2004 PMBOK
Organizational Planning	Human Resource Planning
Staff Acquisition	Acquire Project Team
Team Development	Develop Project Team
	Manage Project Team

Project Communications Management

The processes in this knowledge area are related to—you guessed it—communication skills. Communication encompasses much more than just a simple exchange of information. The Project Communications Management knowledge area ensures that all project information—including project plans, risk assessments, risk response plans, meeting notes, project status, and more—are collected, documented, distributed, and archived at appropriate times. Project managers use communication skills on a daily basis. According to some statistics (and most of you can attest to this from first-hand experience), project managers spend 90 percent of their time communicating. The processes that constitute Project Communications Management include the following:

2000 PMBOK	2004 PMBOK
Communication Planning	Communications Planning
Information Distribution	Information Distribution
Performance Reporting	Performance Reporting
Administrative Closure	Manage Stakeholders

Project Risk Management

The Project Risk Management knowledge area deals with identifying, analyzing, and planning for potential risks. This includes minimizing the likelihood of risk events occurring, minimizing risk consequences, and exploiting positive risks that may improve project performance or outcomes. The processes that constitute Project Risk Management include the following:

2000 PMBOK	2004 PMBOK
Risk Management Planning	Risk Management Planning
Risk Identification	Risk Identification
Qualitative Risk Analysis	Qualitative Risk Analysis
Quantitative Risk Analysis	Quantitative Risk Analysis
Risk Response Planning	Risk Response Planning
Risk Monitoring and Control	Risk Monitoring and Control

Project Procurement Management

The Project Procurement Management knowledge area concerns the purchasing of goods or services from external vendors, contractors, and suppliers. These processes deal with preparing requests for information from contractors, evaluating responses, and selecting the contractor to perform the work or supply the goods. It also deals with contract administration and contract closeout. The processes that constitute Project Procurement Management include the following:

2000 PMBOK	2004 PMBOK
Procurement Planning	Plan Purchases and Acquisitions
Solicitation Planning	Plan Contracting
Solicitation	Request Seller Responses
Source Selection	Select Sellers
Contract Administration	Contract Administration
Contract Closeout	Contract Closure

APPENDIX B

Project Planning Templates

Your life as a project manager can be quite challenging. As you perfect your skills you find tools and techniques that work for you. Then you incorporate them into your project managerment tool belt for use on the next project. I have provided here a set of templates for your future use. You'll can also find them for download at www.harborlightpress.com or www.sybex.com. I hope you find them to be great additions to your project management tool belt.

Planning Reflection

Project Title:_____   Project Manager:_____

Process History: *List other projects that you may be able to use as a template for this project.*

Project Sponsor: *Describe the project sponsor, your relationship with the sponsor, and their ability to support this project.*

Resources: *List the resources that you will need to complete the project. Identify any obstacles to obtaining the resources such as reorganizations or other projects.*

Project Team: *Describe the high-level purpose of the procedure.*

Budget: *Describe the project budget situation.*

Expectations: *Describe any tangible or intangible expectations that you know of for this project.*

Planning Reflection *(continued)*

Project Title:_____   Project Manager:_____

Project Duration: *Identify how long you think the project will take from today to project closeout.*

PM Commitment: *Plan how much time and energy you will need to spend to manage this project.*

Stakeholders: *List the stakeholders of the project. Include their influence and impact on the project (either positive or negative).*

Communication: *Define your personal communication preferences including project documentation and meetings.*

Risk: *Describe the risks that you can currently identify for this project.*

Research: *Describe any research that you will need to perform to manage this project.*

PM Instinct: *Describe what your instinct is telling you about this project.*

Project Scope Statement

Project Title:_____   Project Manager:_____

Purpose: *Provide a high-level, one-line description of the project.*

Project Objectives: *List the corporate business objectives that the project will support.*

Business Justification: *Provide the reason the business took on the project.*

Team Goals: *List the goals the individual team members expect to achieve as a result of finishing this project, such as increased proficiency in a technology or process.*

Project Goals: *List the ends or final purposes of the project defined as SMART goals.*

Critical Success Factors: *List the items you absolutely, positively must have in place for the project to be successful.*

Assumptions: *List the project assumptions. Suggested areas are:*

   Priority

   Resources

   Vendors

   Equipment

   Regulatory environment

   Team stability

   Scope stability

Project Scope Statement *(continued)*

Project Title:_____ Project Manager:_____

Scope:	*List the boundaries of your project. These boundaries need to be clear enough to be the basis of all project decisions; they're what you'll use to manage the project and its deliverables.*

Not in Scope:	*Define what is not in scope or what will be done in another phase.*

Deliverables:	*List the items that will be delivered as part of the project.*

Requirements:	*Collect the project requirements that are the characteristics of the deliverables. Identify where the list will be stored.*

Define Scope Management plan:	*Describe your scope management plan, including scope change management process.*

Scope Statement Approvals:

Risk Management Plan

Project Title:_____   Project Manager:_____

Methodology: *Define the methodology that will be followed for managing risk for the project. This includes the process to identify risks, document the impact, and develop the risk response.*

Roles and Responsibilities: *Define the roles and responsibilities for risk management for the project, including who will identify risks, who will score and interpret the risks, who will create the risk responses, and who will update and publish risk matrices.*

Analysis: *Define the analysis process for the risks. This includes the scoring method that defines the impact and probability of each risk. For example, you can apply a simple value of High, Medium, or Low to each risk impact and probability. This section also includes the formula to determine the risk score.*

Threshold: *Define the method that will be used to identify which risks will be continually monitored and which will be reviewed periodically.*

Budgeting: *Define how the budget impact of risk will be identified and entered into the project budget.*

Reporting: *Define the risk analysis matrix format. List the location where it will be maintained and the frequency of distribution. Define the format of risk reporting if you need to maintain risk lists on executive dashboards.*

Monitor and Control: *Define how each risk will be monitored throughout the project. Each risk will have a team member responsible to monitor and report on the status. Describe the process to identify a new risk, to revise risk scores, and/or to escalate a risk that reaches its triggers.*

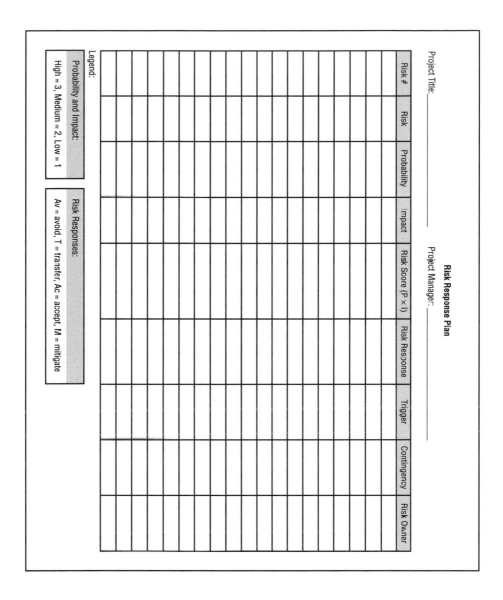

Risk Response Plan

Project Title: _____

Project Manager: _____

Risk #	Risk	Probality	Impact	Risk Score (P × I)	Risk Response	Trigger	Contingency	Risk Owner

Legend:

Probability and Impact:
High = 3, Medium = 2, Low = 1

Risk Responses:
Av = avoid, T = transfer, Ac = accept, M = mitigate

Team Selection Template

Project Title:_____   Project Manager: _____

Sposor:_____

Company Organization:	*Describe the company organization, including functional vs. matrixed. Does the company have a personality test preference? How will you obtain any results?*

Company Culture:	*Describe the company culture with respect to work ethics and team selection processes.*

Project Training:	*Describe the expectation for project training. Include allotted budget or time constraints.*

Hard Skill Matrix

Task	Skill Required	Skill Level (H-M-L)	Number of Employees Needed	Assigned Team Members

Team Selection Template *(continued)*

Project Title:_____   Project Manager: _____

Sposor:_____

Soft Skills Matrix

Team Member	Thinking Preference	Communication Style	Organization Skills	Process Skills

Project Team Role Matrix

Team Member	Role	Department	Phone	E-mail
	Sponsor			
	Project Manager			
	Team Member			
	Stakeholder			
	Subject Matter Experts			

Responsibility Matrix

Activity	Author	Approver	Copy

Communication Management Plan

Project Title:_____   Project Sponsor: _____

Project Manager:_____   Project Team:_____

Activity Communication Plan

Activity	Author/Facilitator	Approver/ Attendees	Copy	Method and Frequency

Define Escalation Strategy:	*Define when an issue will be escalated, such as 48 hours after it was identified. List the people in the escalation channel.*

Location of Project Documentation:	*This should be in one place, whether it's a project notebook or a folder on the network.*

General Meeting Rules:	*List the meeting rules for the project team.*

General Communication Rules:	*List the general communication rules for the project team, including e-mail, phone messages, and telephone or video conferencing. Include the method for notifying PM of issues, status, risks, project date issues, and meetings.*

Budget Spreadsheet

Project Title:_____   Project Manager:_____

Task ID	Description	Estimate				Comments
Task Number from WBS	Task description	Labor			Materials	
		Hrs	Rate	($)	($)	
	Subtotal					
	Total					

Labor rate/s: *Identify the labor rate/s that will be applied to the labor hours. Include how/if you will incorporate benefits into the labor estimate.*

Overhead: *Identify how you will incorporate overhead and administrative costs into the project total (including facility, management, telephone, internet charges, office supplies).*

Miscellaneous: *Include expenses for marketing costs (including collateral or focus groups), legal costs (contracts, patents, trademarks), travel and food, advertising, and training.*

Contingency Reserve: *Identify how you will incorporate contingency reserves into the budget.*

Capital: *Identify if you need to obtain capital dollars for this project.*

Total Project Budget: *Add up all of the costs to successfully complete the project.*

Approval: *Sponsor approval and date for project budget.*

Project Procedure Template

Project Title:_____   Project Manager:_____

Purpose: *Describe the high-level purpose of the procedure.*

Change Log: *Identify the changes to the procedure including author, date, and change.*

Reference Documents: *List other documents that can be used as reference for this procedure.*

Responsibilities: *Define the responsibilities for the procedure including who will manage the changes, who has approval authority, who will use the procedure and who will ensure that the procedure is followed.*

Policies and Guidelines: *Describe any company policies or guidelines that must be followed in addition to this procedure.*

Project Procedure Template *(continued)*

Project Title:_____   Project Manager:_____

Flow Chart for Procedure: *Create a flow chart that matches the steps in the procedure. Make sure the numbering in the procedure steps matches the steps in the flow chart.*

Procedure Steps: *Identify each step of the procedure including who will perform the step. Complete sentences aren't necessary. Start each step with a verb.*

Forms, Templates, and Reports: *Identify any forms templates or reports that will be created or used with this procedure.*

Definitions and Terminology: *Create a definition table, which defines unique terms used within the procedure or associated forms.*

Approval: *List the approver's name, title, and date of approval.*

Quality Management Plan

Project Title:_____   Project Manager: _____

Quality Assurance: *Describe company quality processes or team-specific quality processes for this project.*

Scope Verification: *Describe the process that will be used to verify that the project meets the scope described in this plan, including any approved scope changes for the project. This may be part of the test plan.*

Documentation Acceptance Criteria: *Define the acceptance criteria for documentation which may include signatures, approved e-mails, or simply that the document exists and is filed in the project folder.*

Work Package Acceptance Criteria: *Define the acceptance criteria for deliverables (including work packages). This may include signatures, approved e-mails, and so on.*

Disaster Recovery and Business Continuity Plan: *Describe the location of the corporate disaster recovery procedure. Describe if and how this will be impacted by the project.*

Process Improvements: *Describe the process improvements that will occur during this project. List any procedure that will be created or revised.*

Audits: *Describe any audits that will occur during this project. List who will perform the audits and when the audits are scheduled.*

Task Analysis

Project Title:_____   Task Evaluator: _____

Task Name:_____   Task Number:_____

| Task Estimates: | *Give the estimated time in hours to complete each activity or work package.* |

Task Comments or Details: *List any comments that pertain to the task or any additional activity details that the evaluator wants to capture with their estimate. This can be used for the analysis portion of the task.*

Assumptions & Risks: *List assumptions associated with the estimates including any risks associated with completing the task.*

Deliverables: *List the deliverables associated with this task.*

Interdependencies: *List any task that needs to be completed prior to initiating this task or any task that is relying on the completion of this task to begin.*

Resources: *List the resources required to complete this task. Include any special skills required.*

Equipment and Supplies: *List any equipment and supplies that are needed to complete the task.*

Milestones: *List the milestones associated with this task.*

Acceptance Criteria: *List the acceptance criteria for this task.*

Approval: *PM or Sponsor approval of task estimate.*

Procurement Management Plan Template

Project Title:_____   Project Manager: _____

Purchasing Contact:	*Identify the purchasing contact you'll be using for this project.*

Purchasing Processes:	*Describe company purchasing processes, or identify the procedure to follow for processes or team-specific quality processes for this project. Identify if you must choose vendors from a company-approved list. Include who will need to approve purchase requisitions.*

RFP Processes:	*Do any of the purchases require an RFP? If so, describe the process. Also describe the evaluation and selection criteria for the RFP.*

Purchasing Requirements:	*Identify any resources or services that will be purchased from outside the performing organization*			
Vendor	Item	Lead Time	Due Date	Est. Cost

Procurement Management Plan Template *(continued)*

Project Title:_____   Project Manager: _____

List any milestones that will be used to make partial payments toward the contract.		
Vendor	Milestone	Estimated Date

Contracts and Attachments:	*Describe any contracts or addendum that need to be negotiated or amended during this project. Identify whether the contract is fixed-price, cost-reimbursable, or time and material. Include whether you need to obtain NDAs for this project.*

Branding, Trademarks, and Service Marks:	*Describe any changes or additional branding that will be required for this project.*

Copyrights:	*Describe any new material or changes to current company literature as a result of this project.*

Patents:	*Describe any new patent applications.*

Project Plan Kickoff Agenda Template

Project Title:_____   Project Manager:_____

Scribe and Timekeeper:_____   Location: _____

Date and Time (Start and End Time): _____

		Who	Time
Meeting Initiation:	*Review agenda, scheduled meeting breaks, and method for collecting issues.*		

		Who	Time
Team Introductions:	*Introduce the project team and stakeholders. This is the place for an icebreaker exercise.*		

		Who	Time
Scope Statement Review:	*Describe the scope of the project, including objectives, justification, team goals, project goals, critical success factors, assumptions, and deliverables. Review the scope management process.*		

		Who	Time
Risk Management Plan Review:	*Review the risk management plan to explain the process for identifying and evaluating risks. Obtain agreement on the process.*		

		Who	Time
Risk Analysis Review:	*Review the risk response plan for the high probability and impact risks.*		

		Who	Time
Role and Responsibility Review:	*Review and obtain agreement for the roles and responsibilities of the project team.*		

Project Plan Kickoff Agenda Template *(continued)*

Project Title:_____   Project Manager:_____

Scribe and Timekeeper:_____   Location: _____

Date and Time (Start and End Time): _____

		Who	Time
Communication Management Plan Review:	*Review the communication management plan. Obtain agreement on the communication rules and escalation process.*		

		Who	Time
Budget Review:	*Describe the task analysis process. Review the budget spreadsheet*		

		Who	Time
Schedule Review:	*Review the schedule at a summary level. Identify the milestones. Identify critical path items and the person responsible for critical path tasks.*		

		Who	Time
Quality Plan Review:	*Review the quality plan for the project. Obtain agreement on the approach and processes. Review any project reviews or audits that have been scheduled for this project. Review any procedures that have been identified for creation or revision.*		

		Who	Time
Procurement Management Plan Review:	*Review the procurement management plan.*		

		Who	Time
Approvals:	*Document attendance at the meeting and obtain formal project plan approval.*		

Glossary

acceptance criteria
When and who will review and approve the work packages based on documented standards.

analogous estimates
High-level approximations that are based on experience and projects that are similar in size to the one being estimated and used for business justification. Also known as top-down estimates.

assumptions
Statements that define actions or situations believed to be true.

auditory learners
People whose learning preference is to learn from verbal explanations, conversations, and storytelling.

boilerplate language
The legal language used in similar documents having a definite meaning in the same context.

bottom-up estimates
Project budget and time assessments performed by the people who are doing the work and are experienced, incorporating their skill at completing the work package and factoring in their availability.

business justification
The reason the business decides to pursue a project.

capital expenditures
Costs that can be capitalized per accounting definitions and added to the value of the business as assets rather than expenses.

check sheets
These charts are quality tools used to check off items that identify areas of potential improvement.

contingency plans
A risk response strategy where the project team creates plans for what the team will do when a risk is realized.

contingency reserves
Additional costs added to the projects for unexpected events.

cost-reimbursable contract
A type of contract in which the buyer reimburses the seller for their actual costs plus a fee for the seller's profit.

crashing
A schedule compression technique where you add more resources to complete the critical path tasks.

critical path
The longest full path on the project schedule.

deliverables
A measurable, tangible, verifiable product or outcome that must be produced during a project.

fast tracking
A schedule compression technique where additional tasks are scheduled to work in parallel.

fishbone analysis diagrams (Ishikawa diagrams)
A quality tool used to identify the root cause of a problem.

fixed-price contract
A type of contract in which the buyer agrees to pay the seller a definite, predetermined price.

float

The amount of time a task can be delayed from its early start date without impacting the completion date. Only tasks that aren't on the critical path can have float.

flow charts

A quality tool used to show the steps in a process.

forming stage

The initial stage of team development where team introductions begin.

functional managers

Managers who are responsible for all the work assigned to the employees, including all their salary rewards and any discipline.

Gantt charts

A Gantt chart is a bar chart. The X axis is a time scale, and the Y axis is used for deliverables, activities, phases and so on. A horizontal bar indicates the start and end of a activity, and so on, relative to the time scale. These charts are often used to display the project task interdependencies and task status.

goals

The final purpose and the finish-line measurements for the project that determine the project success.

gold plating

The process where the project team delivers more than what's required to have a successful project.

graphs

A chart used to spot trends in the data.

histograms

Bar charts created from the project-scheduling programs that enables you to view the use of resources over the duration of the project.

impact rating
A measure of the effect of the risk on the project if the risk were to occur.

initiating
The first project management process group in which an organization commits to perform a project.

intellectual property
A product of the intellect that has commercial value, including trademarks, service marks, copyrights, and patents.

issue
An item or question to be resolved on the project that may include a project team question, a problem, a potential risk, or a to-do.

kinesthetic learners
People whose learning preference requires hands-on experiences.

master agreements
Contracts with vendors that describe the relationship between them and are used for long-term relationships.

matrixed organizations
Organizations where employees report to one functional manager while also reporting to one or more project managers.

milestone
Markers for significant events that occur during a project often captured on the project schedule and with zero duration.

natural teams
A group of people that effortlessly works together well and creates synergy. It's a team made up of members who like each other, respect one another, and communicate easily as a group.

network diagrams
Schematic displays of the logical sequence for completing tasks.

norming stage
The third stage of team development where the team is now comfortable with one another and their own positions, which results in the team successfully accomplishing tasks that meet the project's requirements and goals.

Pareto diagram
Bar charts used to identify potential reasons for a problem based on fact.

patent portfolio
A collection of patents that build upon one another, which creates a niche for a company.

performing stage
The fourth stage of team development where communication flows, creativity abounds, and projects are completed almost effortlessly.

probability rating
The chance that the identified risk will occur.

procedures
Document that defines the steps and responsibilities in a processes.

procurement
The process for purchasing services or materials used to acquire goods or services from outside the performing organization.

product life cycle
The description of the process of how you do the work to make the product.

project life cycle

The description of the process of how you plan and manage the project, including the five process groups of project management: initiating, planning, executing, controlling, and closing out.

project objectives

Descriptions of project scope that support corporate direction.

project plan

The formal, approved document that describes how the project will be managed.

purchase orders

Documents used to purchase standard items from approved vendors.

quantity-based estimates

Estimates that take a known duration for an activity multiplied by the number of times that activity will be done.

requirements

Project statements that define the characteristic of the deliverables that allow you to validate the deliverables and meet the needs of the stakeholders and part of the project scope.

risk management planning

A company process that defines its risk management process.

risk response

The plan of how to respond to each individual risk if and when it may occurs.

risk response planning

The plan created by the PM and project team to respond to and manage identified risks on the project.

risk tolerance

The amount of risk a company is willing to accept to get the expected benefits from the project.

scope

A project description that defines the boundary of the project and is the high-level description of the stakeholders' expectations. This includes all the work required and only the work required to complete the project successfully.

scope creep

The slow addition of tasks and requirements to a project in an uncontrolled manner that may result in the project missing goals and deadlines.

secondary risks

Risks caused by a risk response.

service agreements

Documents used to obtain services from approved vendors.

sponsor

The person who ultimately has decision-making authority and who also has the responsibility over the project budget and the ability to assign resources.

sponsor committee

A group of managers responsible for prioritizing and managing the budgets of many projects.

stakeholders

All the people and organizations who have either a positive or a negative impact on your project, including the sponsor, PM, team, and subject matter experts.

storming stage

The second stage of team development where the group begins to figure out where they fit into the team structure and their role for team success.

team goals

The results the individual team members expect to achieve by the end of the project.

time and material contracts
Type of contract that contains features of both the fixed-price contract and cost-reimbursable contracts.

triggers
Warning flags or activities that indicate that a risk has come or will become active.

triple constraints
A widely used set of project goals that include time, cost, and quality.

visual learners
People whose learning preference is to read the information and apply it to the situation. These people prefer data to be presented in charts, pictures, maps, and graphics to clearly understand the message.

Work Breakdown Structure
A deliverable-oriented grouping of project elements that define a project's total scope.

Index

Note to the reader: Throughout this index **boldfaced** page numbers indicate primary discussions of a topic. *Italicized* page numbers indicate illustrations.

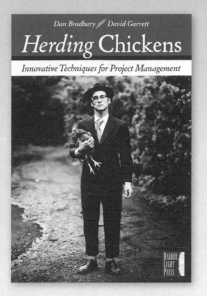
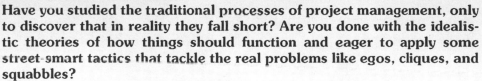

Project Manager's Spotlight Series

The Project Manager's Spotlight series highlights critical components of the project management process and offers clear and concise coverage that is more accessible and applicable than general management titles on the market. The Spotlight Series is written for project managers, team leaders, and team members involved with small-to medium-sized projects on short schedules who are seeking fast, practical solutions to risk management, change management, and/or project planning.

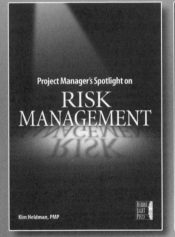

Project Manager's Spotlight on Risk Management

By Kim Heldman, PMP
ISBN: 0-7821-4411-X
Price: US$16.95

Project Manager's Spotlight on Change Management

By Claudia Baca, PMP
ISBN: 0-7821-4410-1
Price: US$16.95

Project Manager's Spotlight on Planning

By Catherine A. Tomczyk, PMP
ISBN: 0-7821-4413-6
Price: US$16.95

Harbor Light Press, an imprint of Sybex, Inc., is dedicated to providing business professionals with the practical skills and innovative solutions needed to succeed in today's competitive workplace.

SYBEX
www.sybex.com

HARBOR LIGHT PRESS